The Art & Life of Georgia O'Keeffe

The Art & Life of

Georgia O'Keeffe

by Jan Garden Castro

Crown Trade Paperbacks, New York

For my grandparents, Anna (1899–1992)
and Rawin Fischer (1883–1984)

For Anita Pollitzer, Ansel Adams, and Lloyd Goodrich

Copyright © 1985, 1995 by Jan Garden Castro
All rights reserved. No part of this book may be reproduced or
transmitted in any form or by any means, electronic or mechanical,
including photocopying, recording, or by any information storage and
retrieval system, without permission in writing from the publisher.
Published by Crown Trade Paperbacks, 201 East 50th Street,
New York, New York 10022. Member of the Crown Publishing Group.
Random House, Inc., New York, Toronto, London, Sydney, Auckland
Crown Trade Paperbacks and colophon are trademarks of Crown Publishers, Inc.
Originally published in hardcover by Crown Publishers, Inc., in 1985.
Manufactured in Italy
Design by Dana Sloan
Library of Congress Cataloging-in-Publication Data
Castro, Jan Garden
The art & life of Georgia O'Keeffe. 1st pb ed.
Bibliography. Includes index.
1. O'Keeffe, Georgia, 1887–1986   2. Painters—
United States—Biography.   I. O'Keeffe, Georgia.
1887–1986.   II. Title.
ND237.O5C3   1995   759.13—dc20   94-42072
[B]
ISBN 0-517-88387-2
10 9 8 7 6 5 4 3 2 1
First Paperback Edition

Contents

Grateful acknowledgment is made to the following:

Amon Carter Museum, Fort Worth, Texas: 85, 112, 134, 147, 154, 163, 165, 167. Doris Bry, photograph by Jack Holmes: 151. Jan Garden Castro: 86, 87, 115, 131. The Cleveland Museum of Art: Bequest of Leonard C. Hanna, Jr.: 28; Hinman B. Hurlbut Collection: 29. Collection of American Literature, the Beinecke Rare Book and Manuscript Library, Yale University: 37, 38, 64. Collection of Mrs. Bernhard G. Bechhoefer, photograph by Mark Gulizian: 129. Collection of Helen W. Boignon, photograph by Sing-Si Schwartz: 65. Collection of the Humanities Research Center, the University of Texas at Austin: 96 (top). Collection of the Museum of Modern Art, New York: 142–143; acquired through the Richard D. Brixey Bequest: 66; Mr. and Mrs. Donald B. Straus Fund: 34. Collection of the New Britain Museum of American Art, Stephen Lawrence Fund, photograph by E. Irving Blomstrann: 73. Collection of the San Diego Museum of Art: Gift of Mrs. Inez Grant Parker in Memory of Earle W. Grant: 48; Gift of Mr. and Mrs. Norton S. Walbridge: 97, 105, 113. Collection of Santa Barbara Museum of Art, Gift of Mrs. Gary Cooper: 137. Collection of Paul and Tina Schmid, photograph by Greg Heins: 33. Collection of Warren and Jane Shapleigh: 69. Collection of the University Art Museum, University of New Mexico, Albuquerque: 13. Collection of the Whitney Museum of American Art, New York: 99. Collection of the Wichita Art Museum, Wichita, Kansas: 60–61. Detroit Institute of Arts, gift of Robert H. Tannahill: 96 (lower). Evans J. Downer: 100. Philippe Halsman: front jacket, 83, 111. Hirshhorn Museum and Sculpture Garden, Smithsonian Institution: 114, 172. Mr. David S. Lifson, photograph by Sing-Si Schwartz: 168. Memorial Art Gallery of the University of Rochester, Marion Stratton Gould Fund: 159. The Metropolitan Museum of Art, Alfred Stieglitz Collection: 10, 51, 59, 146. Milwaukee Art Museum: Collection of Mrs. Harry Lynde Bradley: 4, 5, 21, 25, 77, 124, 132, 148, 152; Gift of Mrs. Edward R. Wehr: 133. Munson-Williams-Proctor Institute, Utica, New York: 136. Museum of Fine Arts, St. Petersburg, Florida, Gift of Charles and Margaret Stevenson in memory of Jeanne Crawford Henderson: 76. National Museum of American Art (formerly National Collection of Fine Arts), Smithsonian Institution, Gift of S. C. Johnson and Son, Inc.: 149; Gift of the Woodward Foundation: 68. Nebraska Art Association, courtesy Sheldon Memorial Art Gallery, University of Nebraska-Lincoln, Thomas C. Woods Collection: 72 (left). Norton Gallery and School of Art, West Palm Beach, Florida: 84, 125; lent anonymously 144–145. Collection of Mrs. John Wintersteen: 26. The Phillips Collection, Washington, D.C.: xiv, 81, 89, 104, 161. Dr. William S. Pollitzer: 23. Private Collections: Courtesy, Andrew Crispo Gallery, Inc., New York: 16, 20, 27, 44, 57, 58, 93, 101 (bottom), 120, 128, 169, 170; photograph courtesy of James Maroney, New York: 164; 46, 49, 50, 55, 92, 103, 151. The Regis Collection: 45, 72 (right), 109, 141, 156, 160. The St. Louis Art Museum: 158; Gift of Charles E. Claggett in memory of Blanche Fischel Claggett: 63; Gift of Charles E. and Mary Merrill: 91; Gift of Mrs. Ernest W. Stix: 43. San Francisco Museum of Modern Art: 138; Gift of Hamilton-Wells Collection, photograph by Don Meyer: 108; Gift of Charlotte Mack, photograph by Don Meyer: 80. Thyssen-Bornemisza Collection, Lugano, Switzerland: 101 (top), 153. The Trustees of the Ansel Adams Publishing Rights Trust, photograph © 1984: 78. University of Arizona Museum of Art, Gift of Oliver James: 53. Mrs. Patricia Young: 9, 40.

Acknowledgments

This book has been a ten-year effort. It began when artist/teacher Peggy Grant showed me O'Keeffe's work. In 1976, I showed my forty-six-page monograph on O'Keeffe's art to St. Louis Art Museum Director James D. Burke and lecturer Alexandra Bellos. The monograph was favorably received, with the need for an extensive study recognized and encouraged. Next I spent four months at the Beinecke Rare Book and Manuscript Library at Yale University reading the voluminous correspondence and documents in the Alfred Stieglitz Collection and Archives, down to the Wastebasket Collection.[1] The rich documentary materials, as well as other scholars studying the same materials, provided further leads which I followed throughout the East, the Southeast, the South, and across the country to the Southwest and West Coast. I studied many unpublished documentary materials and many original works of art by O'Keeffe in public and private collections.

During the course of my research and writing, I have been most grateful for cooperation and suggestions from museum directors, curators, art historians, artists, photographers, and individuals who have firsthand information about O'Keeffe's art and life. Those who have facilitated my completion of the book include Donald Gallup, former Curator of the Collection of American Literature at The Beinecke Rare Book and Manuscript Library and present Curator David Schoonover; Garnett McCoy, Archivist at the Archives of American Art; Beaumont Newhall, first Curator of Photography at the Museum of Modern Art; Lloyd Goodrich, former Director of the Whitney Museum of American Art; photographer Ansel Adams; Dr. Evan Turner, Director of the Cleveland Museum of Art; George Neubert, Director of the Sheldon Memorial Art Gallery; James Burke, Director of the St. Louis Art Museum; Martin E. Petersen, Curator of Paintings at the San Diego Museum of Art; Robert Hall and Pearl Creswell, Curator and staff member of Fisk Memorial Gallery, Fisk University; Weston Naef, Curator of Photography at the Metropolitan Museum; Peter Bunnell, Professor of the History of Photography, Princeton University; photography and art connoisseurs David Hunter McAlpin, Myron Kunin, and Elsie Dewald; artist Robert Dash; writers Dorothy Norman and Michael Castro; art historians Sarah Greenough, Naomi Rosenblum, Sherrye Cohn, and Nelson Wu, my mentor; biographer Sue Davidson Lowe; museum staff members Anita Duquette, Mary Ann Steiner, Patti Nelson, and Jane Collins; and all other curators and staff at museums lending works, including the National Gallery of Art, the National Museum of American Art, the Archives of American Art, the Metropolitan Museum of Art, the Art Institute of Chicago, the Amon Carter Museum of Western Art, the Whitney Museum of American Art, the San Francisco Museum of Modern Art, the Norton Gallery and School of Art, and the Santa Barbara Museum of Art; Dr. William S. Pollitzer; Lisa Healy, my editor at Crown; attorney Gustin Reichbach; agent Mary Yost; my son Jomo; and my professional associates, friends, and family.

I have written the following pages with the same dedication to "seeing" that O'Keeffe has brought to her finest art. My primary intention is to bring together field research, including historical materials that might otherwise be lost, to pay tribute to the living art of the twentieth century's legendary, iron-willed artist. O'Keeffe's mystique is awesome but not impenetrable.

This book is dedicated to my beloved grandparents, of O'Keeffe's generation; my grandma's opinions of O'Keeffe and my grandpa's grace at age one hundred add to my understanding of the artist and the aging process. This dedication extends to art historian Lloyd Goodrich and to O'Keeffe's deceased friends Anita Pollitzer and Ansel Adams, all of whom have given me important insights about O'Keeffe's art. I thank Adams and Goodrich for their distinguished contributions in the fields of photography and art history and all the dedicatees for their generosity of spirit and integrity which have taught me enduring American qualities that I emulate and admire.

A New Introduction to O'Keeffe's Creation

Advance orders helped *The Art & Life of Georgia O'Keeffe* gain best-seller standing upon its publication in November 1985, the month of the artist's ninety-eighth birthday. Among the distinguished authors contributing positive comments and reviews, Howard Nemerov, America's Poet Laureate, wrote:

As well as being a splendid production of a book, a pleasure to hold and look through, this is an essay beautifully conceived, executed, illustrated. Jan Castro has achieved a happy harmony of biography, scholarship, and criticism, and offered the readers a fine illumination of both the life and the work of the artist whose greatest natural gift has been so fully realized.

Despite a flurry of publishing activity since her death in March 1986, many of O'Keeffe's secrets and her enigma have survived the scrutiny of more recent biographies and critical studies largely because her celebrated friends respected confidences from (and about) the artist, as I respected their confidences to me. After examining and reflecting upon facts culled from ten years of research, I included pertinent, then-little-known biographical details in the text and notes. I crafted my prose to match the artist's pared-down, yet revealing visual language. My original analyses of O'Keeffe's art and her words, and of varied critics' perspectives—from feminist to sexist—remain valid.

What lies ahead for O'Keeffe's legacy? In the future, Barbara Buhler Lynes's definitive catalogue should solidify the artist's reputation. Another text, *From the Faraway Nearby: Georgia O'Keeffe as Icon,* features twenty viewpoints written after O'Keeffe's death. Cumulatively, they confirm that the artist imposed her exacting standards on subordinates and that gender contributed to various circumstances she faced as an artist, as the subject of art writing, and as an octogenarian. These short chronicles, ranging from O'Keeffe's treatment by male critics in the 1920s to John Poling's report about painting some of O'Keeffe's last works, largely corroborate the contextualized accounts in this book but may inadvertently validate some biased readings of O'Keeffe's life.

The Art & Life of Georgia O'Keeffe combines biographical and art historical approaches but disagrees with those in either discipline who position O'Keeffe within Oriental, Transcendental, Freudian, photographic, realist, minimalist, or other movements popular throughout her long life. I concur with Lloyd Goodrich's quoted view that O'Keeffe's originality is paramount. Using invariably quirky humor and perspectives, she painted each object into "a living thing" to carve out an indomitable style.

The Art & Life of Georgia O'Keeffe

Red Hills and the Sun, Lake George, *1927, oil on canvas, 27" x 32"*

1. Buggy Wheels in the Dust

Georgia O'Keeffe has become a legend in her own time, yet the origins of the myths about her have never been explored. What is O'Keeffe's mystique? When did it begin? Why has she remained so reclusive, so unwilling to let the public see the full range of her prodigious artistic creations? Why did she make her home in the remote desert mesas of the American Southwest? How has she become an American heroine in her own time? As an artist, what have been some of her guiding principles?

The answers to these and other questions revolve around a closer study of the visual aspects of her art. O'Keeffe's *way of seeing*—her deep appreciation of nature synthesized in works of art—is unique. She pursued her vision when she was unknown, when she was the only American-educated woman in the select group of European-educated male artists exhibited by Alfred Stieglitz in the twenties, and when she found her home in the American Southwest. O'Keeffe's art contains richly colored forms—abstract shapes, flowers, buildings, bones, hills, trees, clouds, sky, and stones—variously characterized in large, clean patterns that are now her trademark. The brilliant, but sometimes uneven, quality of her work and her innovations in technique, theme, and style are central to her remarkable career as an artist.

Just as Pablo Picasso's achievements are now being seen comprehensively for the first time, O'Keeffe's entire *oeuvre* has a cumulative visual richness that deserves study. Her work, so large and accessible to the viewer, has subtle abstract and geometric properties, new insights into the use of color and form, and bold thematic and social concerns. During a life that spans the twentieth century, O'Keeffe has had the courage to focus on the contradictions and greatness of America *as she sees it*.

O'Keeffe's early perceptions of the things around her were in colors, shapes, and textures. In her book *Georgia O'Keeffe,* she recalls seeing light on a red, white, and black patterned quilt before she could walk, and, as a toddler, the soft, smooth shapes made by buggy wheels in the dust—they looked good enough to eat! She also worked intensively trying to draw a man. He was bending over from the hip like her miniature china dolls, but she never quite got his shape right. Turning the drawing over, she was delighted when the man now appeared to be on his back with his legs up!

Georgia Totto O'Keeffe, born on November 15, 1887, in Sun Prairie, Wisconsin, was the first female offspring of Francis and Ida O'Keeffe. She was named after her fondly remembered Hungarian grandfather, George Victor Totto, but never used her middle name; nor did she pass on the family stories about George Victor. In fact, as she grew up, she discouraged stories by others about her family history, childhood, and early life to an unusual degree—with the result that recollections about the young Georgia come primarily from the remarkably precise memories of the artist herself.

These reveal the significant traits which the artist retained from childhood. Her two grandmothers had commanding personalities. Grandmother Totto, who lived in Madison, was a "tall dignified woman, beautiful in bearing, with masses of white hair and most particular ways."[1] One of those ways was a distinctive manner of speaking. When she told the children not to touch the collection of fine ornaments in the parlor, Georgia recalled, "I was so fascinated by her precise way of speaking that I would do it again just to hear her say, 'You must not do that a-gain.'"[2] However, Georgia preferred the elegant name of her other grandmother, Mary Catherine O'Keeffe, to hers. Catherine's hair was usually braided around her head; she wore blue at home and black when she came to visit. The mature artist's habits of wearing black with white collars or other one-toned suits, keeping her silver hair plaited or pinned at the nape of her neck, having ramrod posture, speaking precisely, and assembling collections of "untouchable" ornaments from nature, all may stem from the conscious and subconscious influence of her two grandmothers.[3]

At an early age, she enjoyed working with her hands. One project, sewing tiny clothes for her china dolls, was undoubtedly influenced by Grandma Catherine's skill at fine sewing and the example that most of her garments, including underwear, were handmade. O'Keeffe improvised a portable dollhouse—two intersecting flats of cardboard that made four "rooms," and could be carried to an outdoor terrain—a sand walk, and weed "trees." Her intimate recall of these early projects establishes her active imagination as a child and her independence in pursuing them.[4] Later, as a student and teacher, O'Keeffe made some of her own clothes by hand; as a successful artist, she began to order clothes to fit her own "most particular" style.

Georgia O'Keeffe was a loner, even as one of seven children growing up on the large, bustling dairy farm in Sun Prairie. Her parents had grown up on neighboring farms that had been combined at their marriage. Ida Ten Eyck Totto was twenty when she married Francis O'Keeffe in Madison, Wisconsin, on February 19, 1884. As Francis worked to expand their holdings to six hundred acres of fertile country land, there was plenty of space for the children, born within a few years of each other: Francis, Georgia, Ida, Anita, Alexis, Catherine, and Claudia.

Georgia's father, Francis, had left home in his twenties to explore the Dakotas and seek better prospects, just as his parents had left Ireland for America. Pierce O'Keeffe of County Cork and Catherine Shortal of Kilkenny had been forced to abandon the family's formerly profitable wool business after the imposition of severe tariffs. In 1848, the O'Keeffes traveled by boat from Liverpool to New York, and from the Great Lakes to Milwaukee, then by oxcart to Wisconsin. They purchased land three and a half miles from Sun Prairie and twelve and a half miles from Madison—a remote spot in horse-and-buggy days. They planted potatoes, corn, and turnips; built the first frame house in the area; and raised four sons: Bernard, Francis, Boniface, and Peter. Francis was jovial, easygoing, and the one in the family with curly hair. The O'Keeffes were Catholics; Pierce and Catherine made the long drive to church on Sundays in their Irish finery—Pierce in a high hat and fine worsted suit and Catherine in a dress of watered silk and a flowered hat, with a purple parasol.

Georgia's mother came from Puritan, Dutch, and Hungarian stock. On her mother's paternal side, Georgia descended from Coenradt Ten Eyck, who emigrated from Holland around 1650 to become a founder of the Dutch Reform Church in the New World. On her mother's maternal side, she was a ninth-generation direct descendant of Edward Fuller, a signer of the Mayflower Compact for the ship's maiden voyage to America in 1620. Her great grand-father, Charles Wyckoff, owned the then-famous National Hotel on Cortlandt Street in New York City from 1838 until 1846. He eventually moved west to Wisconsin. There, his daughter, Isabell Dunham Wyckoff, met and married George Victor Totto, a count from Budapest and the aide-de-camp of Lajos Kossuth, leader of Hungary's 1848 revolution against Austria. In exile, Totto lived at the Wyckoff's National Hotel. He moved to Wisconsin after his friend, Count Haraszthy, bought a ten-thousand-acre tract and founded a Hungarian settlement devoted to the democratic way of life. This became Sauk City, where George Victor Totto and Isabell Dunham Wyckoff were married on May 21, 1855. Among their six children was a daughter Ida, who was Georgia's mother.

As the Tottos and the O'Keeffes were raising their children in Sun Prairie, the rest of the community was growing as well. Sun Prairie, originally near an Indian trail from Koshkonong to Fort Winnebago, had been named in 1837 when a journeying party discovered the sun-filled plain and left the words "Sun Prairie" carved upon a great oak. Wisconsin became a state in 1848, and the railroad came in 1859; both events facilitated the growth of the small town into a grain market. The town, incorporated in 1868, grew to eight hundred by 1877. But town life and farm life were still provincial in comparison with George's life in Hungary, and he became restless. In the 1880s, he took a business trip home, confirmed that his banishment had ended, and remained in his native country. Isabell stoically coped with her husband's desertion. Yet she was unable to manage the farm without him, so she reluctantly moved her family to Madison. She regarded George as a hero in spite of his permanent departure.

In the meantime, Francis O'Keeffe was urged to return home by his widowed mother Catherine. If Francis made a match with Ida Totto, both families would benefit, and their neighboring property could be consolidated. Two of her sons had died of tuberculosis, and Boniface was not strong. A man was needed on the farm. Their union suited both husbandless matriarchs. The Tottos' Episcopal clergyman, Reverend J. B. Pratt, officiated at the Totto house in Madison. After the birth of the young married couple's first son, also named Francis, Isabell's sister came from Madison for a visit and never left. She was called Auntie by the children she helped to raise.

The two grandmothers, Auntie, and Ida brought a matriarchal style to the busy farm; the big white frame house was a center of activity. The family, the farm help, and the local teacher all ate together and lived in the big house, yet went their own ways. Francis was at work from early morning until dark overseeing the dairy he had started and other farm chores.

A mingling of Irish, English, and American music, art, and literature were all early cultural experiences for young Georgia. Her father played Irish airs such as "The Black Bird" and "Galway Bay" on the fiddle, and the girls were expected to learn to play the piano.

At about age eleven, Georgia and two younger sisters studied art with a local woman who supervised the lessons about cubes, perspective, shading, and detail in the Prang drawing book. The following year, the girls were driven to Sun Prairie on Saturdays to study with a local artist, Mrs. Mann. They copied pictures again, but Georgia also learned to work in watercolor. In her book *Georgia O'Keeffe,* she describes two favorites—a lighthouse at sea which was imagined and a tall, pointed spruce against the snow which she could see from the teacher's house. For Georgia, the real excitement came from working out the technical challenges of perspective, lighting, and white snow on her own while the teacher was occupied.[5]

One art influence came from an adult book. Mrs. Crippen, a

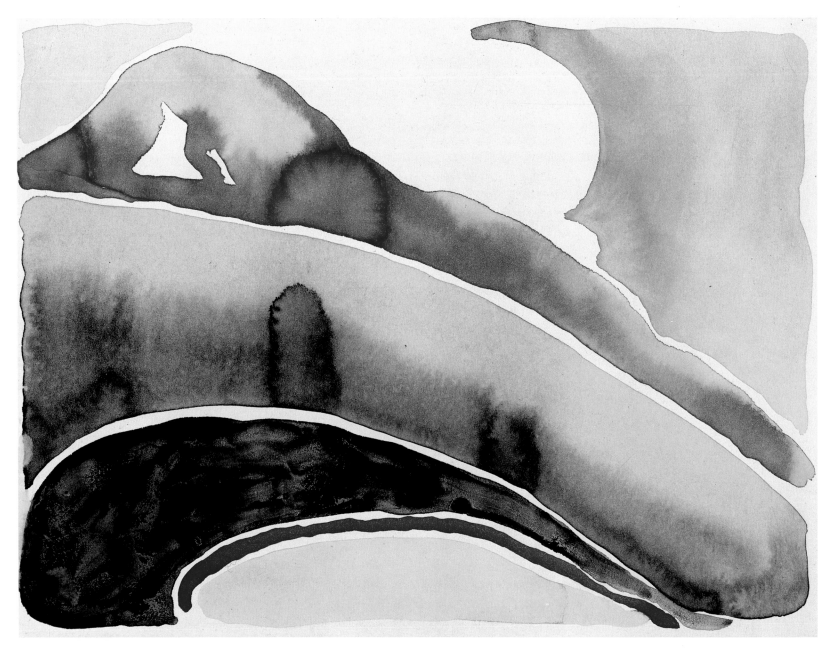

Pink and Green Mountains III, *1917, watercolor on paper, 9" x 12"*

The Flag, *1918, watercolor on paper, 11⅞" x 8¾"*

neighbor several miles down the road, frequently exchanged books with Mrs. O'Keeffe. One of her books contained a two-inch-high pen-and-ink drawing of a girl with beads around her neck titled "Maid of Athens." When Georgia looked back to this time, she noted, "I believe that picture started something moving in me that has had to do with the everlasting urge that makes me keep on painting."[6] Around this time, thirteen-year-old Georgia told the washerwoman's daughter Lena, who had no idea what *she* was going to grow up to be, "*I'm* going to be an artist."[7] In her young life, highly disciplined compared to that of most children today, art already provided an outlet for her creative and imaginative sensibilities.

Throughout her youth, literature reinforced her artistic outlook by providing action-packed stories of history, adventure, and travel. On rainy days and often at night, her mother would read to the oldest son Francis, who had weak eyes, and the other children: *The Life of Hannibal,* Stanley's *Adventures in Africa,* all of *The Leatherstocking Tales,* the Bible, *Pilgrim's Progress, Arabian Nights, The Life of Kit Carson,* and Wild West stories of cattlemen, buffalo, and Indians. As an adult, O'Keeffe's adventures in the Wild West have some remarkable correspondences to these tales, and also grew into legends for the next generation.

In the meantime, nature was the private, personal domain of the curious, independent child. Georgia walked to school each day, in all but the most inclement weather, along the apple orchard. Fields of grain, great oak trees, rough-tongued cows, and clammy-skinned frogs—every detail of nature became familiar to Georgia. She often played alone in a low place in the meadow with the blue sky overhead. In spring, she went with her class to the woods to pick wild flowers for May baskets.

In comparison to the vast plains with her own secret places, the one-room schoolhouse just beyond the farm was cramped, and the lessons were boring. Georgia's elementary schoolteacher, Mrs. Zed Edison, recalled that Georgia was a loner who sometimes popped up with curious questions: "If the lake near us rose up, way up, and spilled all over, how many people would be drowned?" If the answer didn't satisfy her pupil, the child would reply that she'd ask her Aunt Lola, a schoolteacher in Madison. Georgia learned to read early, but she always had trouble with spelling. She repeated the last grade because her mother didn't want to send her to the school in town.[8]

Ida sternly supervised the lives of her children. They could not go to other children's houses to play but could invite friends over. Georgia later imitated the authoritative, perfectionist manner of her mother, who seemed to give more attention to the other children, especially the nearsighted Francis and the darling, Anita. Ida's ability to manage the busy household and to enjoy social and cultural activities with friends was carefully noted by her oldest daughter, who, nevertheless, kept her distance from the socializing.

Instead of childhood memories of friends, siblings, and other human experiences, Georgia told later friends about prized objects that appealed to her quick eye and mind. Their house had the first telephone line—before it reached Sun Prairie—with the telephone in the dining room by the window. Her bedroom had furniture painted gray with blue trim; the bed headboard was decorated with a pink rose and pansies. "Home" for O'Keeffe meant her own room; art, books, and music; the phone; the apple orchard, garden, and barn; and homemade ice cream.

The same summer that she decided, on her own, to be an artist, her parents decided, without consulting her, to send her to Sacred Heart Academy to continue her education. This Dominican convent school was twelve miles from Madison. The woods and lake surrounding the convent and the drawing studio on the top floor became favorite haunts. For the first time, Georgia also excelled in academic subjects, such as English and history. Her first drawings of model casts were small and black, so Sister Angelique drew on top of them with large, light strokes. By following her teacher's suggestions, she won the medal in drawing at the end of the year. The winning drawing was also her first publication. Ida, who never pampered her oldest daughter, is reported to have remarked, "Why shouldn't you get a medal? I would be surprised if you didn't."[9]

The following year Georgia was sent to Madison to live on Lake Mendota at the house of her mother's two unmarried sisters, Lola Totto, a teacher, and Miss Ollie, a librarian. One day at school, the art teacher, whom she remembered as a thin woman wearing a bonnet with artificial purple violets, taught her to look closely at jack-in-the-pulpit flowers. Flowers were already one of O'Keeffe's favorite subjects, and the lesson sparked a lasting interest in flower detail. She studied the jack's strange shapes, the variations in color—deep earthy violet through heavy greens, the purplish hood or flap, and the inner seeds. Ten years later, O'Keeffe created a series of jacks that began with a realistic portrait of the full flower. Each succeeding canvas focused at close range on parts of the jack, resulting in images that moved dramatically beyond realism to explore abstract qualities of the leaf and flower. This attention and appreciation of aspects of nature that ordinary observers take for granted, or never see, began in her youth, yet only after O'Keeffe became familiar with the ideas of Arthur Dow, Wassily Kandinsky, and Alfred Stieglitz did she begin to transform nature according to her inner vision.

In 1902, the O'Keeffe family was in the process of selling the farm and moving to Williamsburg, Virginia. The move to a warmer climate was on behalf of their overworked, unwell father whose last brother had died, like the other two, of tuberculosis. Although their new frame house was larger than the one in Sun Prairie, the moving process was stressful for both parents.

In Williamsburg for summer vacation, Georgia spent her time exploring the southern town—the early cry of the oysterman bringing his catch from the nearby James River, sweet potato pie, and the countryside. Ida adapted easily to the manners, mores, and traditions of the South while Francis, lacking education and sophistication, did not. His business projects were not going well. But for now, this didn't interrupt the children's lives: school be-

gan again. The oldest son, Francis, was to attend the nearby College of William and Mary, her sisters Anita and Ida were enrolled in public schools in town, and Georgia was to attend Chatham Episcopal Institute, a boarding school in a country setting between Danville and Lynchburg.

At Chatham, O'Keeffe was noticeably different from the southern girls. She wore a loose-fitting, plain tailored suit instead of the small-waisted, tight, frilly dresses that were fashionable; her hair was drawn back from her forehead and braided rather than puffed out in a beribboned pompadour. She kept her talk plain in the midst of all the southern accents.

Because O'Keeffe was already talented and independent, she soon won acceptance from the other girls despite her differences. During her two years at Chatham, she learned to play the piano better, but not to spell better. O'Keeffe came dangerously close to flunking out due to her original spelling habits. She often took long walks toward the "beckoning" Blue Ridge Mountains. She taught some girls how to play poker, an unauthorized game, and was fond of practical jokes; these pastimes earned her enough demerits to jeopardize her graduation. Because of her pranks, nerve, and talent, she was quite popular with her peers. Georgia O'Keeffe stories were often on the tongues of the other students. This was the beginning of legends about her.

O'Keeffe also won a lifetime friend at Chatham—the principal and art teacher, Mrs. May Willis. O'Keeffe was able to draw and paint freehand at her own table in art class while most of the other girls worked on china painting. Sometimes she did quick caricatures which she crumpled up, saying, "I don't want any of those pictures floating around to haunt me in my later years."[10] She worked with great freedom in watercolors, using the wet-paper method and Whatman paper. The school kept her best painting, a large watercolor of red and yellow corn. A bunch of purple lilacs was another remembered favorite.

O'Keeffe also became art editor of the school yearbook, *The Mortar-Board.* She selected simple, humorous art by others. Her own art, a featured attraction, included a black-faced tambourine player marching with his flower-shaped black shadow; six black dancers with white shadows and highlights; and caricatures of specific teachers. One teacher is holding her nose as she remarks, "Young ladies, H₂S has a very disagreeable odor." The joke, referring to the rotten-egg smell of a lab chemical, was self-evident to her classmates. Humor, movement, and the dramatic use of black and white give these early works vitality. The other *Mortar-Board* editors made up these two mottos for Georgia Totto O'Keeffe:

A girl who would be different in
habit, style, and dress,
A girl who doesn't give a cent for
men—and boys still less.

O is for O'Keeffe, an artist divine;
Her paintings are perfect and her drawings
are fine.[11]

The class poems about O'Keeffe were on target—she *had* already given her heart to art. Mrs. Willis encouraged her favorite student to continue her studies at the Art Institute of Chicago. After graduating from Chatham in 1905, she entered the Institute that fall.

This was the last summer that her family lived in the big frame house. O'Keeffe saw that her father was demoralized because he had not been able to farm the land. His business ventures—a grocery, then a molding-machine operation that turned shells into construction blocks—were failing.

Luckily, her favorite aunts Lola and Ollie and Uncle Charles had moved closer—to Chicago. She stayed with them in 1905, walking to classes at the Art Institute. There, O'Keeffe appreciated most the lectures of the hunchbacked anatomist and draftsman John Vanderpoel, whom she called one of the few true teachers she has ever known. She purchased his book, *The Human Figure,* and admired the large, deft drawings he created on sheets of tan paper as he talked. The school's emphasis on life drawing did not interest her, however, and the drab, poorly lit classrooms, the artificial drawing conditions, and the egotism of male students dampened her spirits. The family outings on Lake Michigan in an old fishing rowboat and an occasional evening at the theater with her uncle were a welcome relief.

The return to Williamsburg confirmed that her family's troubles were increasing. The radiant countryside, alive with jonquils, crocuses, yellow flowering Scotch broom, pink and blue hyacinths, and stars of Bethlehem, contrasted directly with the old house on the York River where the family now lived. To make matters worse, a typhoid epidemic was sweeping through town. O'Keeffe contracted the fever and was seriously ill.

After a slow recovery, she was enrolled in the Art Students League in New York in 1907. Here, O'Keeffe, just twenty, regained some of the inspiration of her school days at Chatham. Classes, city life, and student adventures offered a taste of the art world she now aspired to join. The typhoid fever had caused her long hair to fall out, and it grew back in curls for the first and only time in her life. The students gave her the Irish nickname Patsy, or Pat.

New York City was a booming metropolis at the turn of the century. Critic Lewis Mumford poetically depicted its feverish pitch of activity in an essay, "The Metropolitan Milieu": "After the Civil War, despite the energetic rise of Chicago, New York City became an imperial metropolis, sucking into its own whirlpool the wealth and the wreckage of the rest of the country and of the lands beyond the sea."[12] Mumford contrasted the great men, such as poet Walt Whitman and artist Albert Pinkham Ryder, and the great architectural achievements, such as the completion of the Brooklyn Bridge in 1883, with the loss of open markets, the rise of confining skyscrapers, and the greed for wealth and power. He admired the way his contemporary Alfred Stieglitz had maintained his moral and artistic direction in the midst of the chaotic growth of the City:

The problem for the creative mind in the 'nineties, whether he
was a young writer like Stephen Crane or a young man with a

Untitled (Purple and White Petunias), *date unknown, oil on canvas, 35" x 29⅜"*

Alfred Stieglitz at "291" *by Edward J. Steichen, 1915, photograph*

passion for photography like Alfred Stieglitz, was to face this New York of boundless misdirected energy and to capture a portion of that wasteful flow for his own purposes, using its force without accepting its habitual channels and its habitual destinations. But there was still another problem: and that was to conquer, with equal resolution, the gentility, the tepid overrefinement, the academic inertness and lack of passionate faith, masquerading as sound judgment, which were characteristic of the stale fugitive culture of the bourgeoisie. The genteel standards that prevailed were worse than no standards at all: dead objects, dead techniques, dead forms of worship, cast a morbid shadow on every enterprise of the mind, making mind itself a sham, causing vitality to seem somehow shameful.[13]

Mumford's admittedly subjective analysis of the conflict between rapid growth and new aesthetic values addresses an issue that indirectly affected the young art student Georgia O'Keeffe. Her classes at the League were progressive in comparison with her previous art education, yet somewhat "stale," in Mumford's sense of the word. Here William Merritt Chase, a nattily dressed, commercially successful portraitist and still-life artist whose technique was an adaptation of European Impressionism, taught O'Keeffe a lasting lesson about detail and style. He showed his students a painting by portraitist John Singer Sargent depicting a gold watch chain in a single brushstroke. Even though the subject matter—the gold watch chain—was of little interest to O'Keeffe, she did master the ability to express detail simply and directly and to incorporate the detail in a larger unified composition. She enjoyed Chase's "dash and go" method of painting one canvas on top of the last with quick, sure brushstrokes. She imitated her teacher's style so well that her *Dead Rabbit with Copper Pot* received a top prize, qualifying her for a scholarship at the League's summer school on Lake George. Within a few years, she would discard this style as imitative, yet she would retain the principle of integrating parts to the whole work. She ultimately went further than her teacher in her ability to use color to express details simply and to incorporate them into a work so that the final picture seemed to have been painted with one grand brushstroke.

The lessons at the League were conservative in comparison with the modern art being shown by Alfred Stieglitz at 291. O'Keeffe went with Eugene Speicher and other League students to see the controversial Rodin drawings. The fifty-eight works, shown from January 2 through 21, 1908, were visceral yet abstract and spare—totally shocking to viewers used to representation, romanticism, or realism. Stieglitz, already a celebrated photographer, was acquiring a blazing reputation as an advocate for the recognition of photography as a fine art in America. He had created and inspired new directions in photography for himself and others, provoking the antagonism of conservative camera buffs. When the Camera Club, which he had helped to found, had voted to expel him, he had sued for reinstatement, then resigned. He had opened his first gallery, the Little Galleries of the Photo-Secession, at 291 Fifth Avenue, in 1905. Called simply "291" by visitors and insiders, the gallery moved next door in 1908; by then, Stieglitz had already been showing painters side by side with photographers for nearly two years. Existing perceptions of modern art were shaken as he introduced the work of Rodin, Matisse, Cézanne, Picasso, and others to a skeptical American public, challenging the whole art world to broaden its visual criteria and change its staid directions. As the League boys gleefully baited Stieglitz to get him to talk about modern art, O'Keeffe withdrew to a back room until the volleys subsided. As she recalled in her book *Georgia O'Keeffe:* "The drawings were curved lines and scratches with a few watercolor washes and didn't look like anything I had been taught about drawing. The teachers at the League thought that Stieglitz might just be fooling the public with the name Rodin, or that Rodin might be fooling both Stieglitz and the public."

As a twenty-year-old in New York for the first time, O'Keeffe would have howled with laughter if anyone suggested that she would marry the famous impresario who was holding court in the other room. Yet the curious art held her attention, despite her perplexity as to how to characterize it.

At this time, O'Keeffe made a personal breakthrough in her technique which she found just as exciting as the classes. O'Keeffe found a way to size and prepare the canvas with "something white" to produce a fresh, bright base. Throughout her career, O'Keeffe paid meticulous attention to her craft; her brushes were always the cleanest, her colors the freshest and brightest among the painters at the League.[14] Yet at this stage, her natural attraction to color was never directly encouraged by teachers. Although Manhattan was becoming an art metropolis, O'Keeffe was almost as isolated, in her love for pure color, as Matisse in rural France. Like Matisse, her color sense would blossom in rural settings— closer to nature.

When O'Keeffe's family could not afford to continue her art education, she returned to Williamsburg that fall. She realized that she needed to contribute to their diminishing resources, and so she worked for two years as a commercial artist in Chicago. Her tedious job, drawing lace and embroidery under the pressure of daily deadlines, ended when she contracted the measles and, as a result, could no longer bear the eyestrain at work.

O'Keeffe returned to Virginia in 1912, but her exact living situation is sketchy. In all likelihood, she first lived with her father in Williamsburg, then the family lived together for a brief period in Charlottesville before Francis went his own way. In 1908 in Williamsburg, her father had built a house of cement and shell blocks molded with his machinery. The dwelling, characterized as a coffin by one neighbor, was a sad metaphor for the family's situation. Ida and Francis separated shortly thereafter—a fact O'Keeffe never discussed with anyone. Her mother and sisters had moved to Charlottesville around 1909, renting a house near the University of Virginia. Ida, although ill with tuberculosis, had relocated to escape the family's worsening situation in Williamsburg and so that her daughters Anita and Claudia could attend classes at the

University. Ida and her daughters subsisted by taking in student boarders. Francis O'Keeffe moved to Charlottesville around 1912 and opened a creamery. Although the family appeared to be reunited, the adult members had already begun to go their own ways.[15] The family's unstable living situation contributed to O'Keeffe's lack of inspiration, and she appeared to have abandoned her dream of becoming an artist from 1908 until 1912.

Her sister Claudia, however, encouraged her to visit the summer art class of Alon Bement, a professor of fine arts at Columbia Teachers' College in New York who headed the University of Virginia art faculty each summer. O'Keeffe enrolled in Bement's class and was introduced to the art principles of Bement's mentor, Arthur Dow. That summer, as she renewed her facility, her determination to become an artist returned. Art not only refueled O'Keeffe's imagination; it also allowed her to suppress morbid reminders of her immediate reality.

Dow's approach was basic and design-oriented. This educator, dissatisfied with academic art studies in France, had formulated an Americanized approach to color and composition in his book, *Composition,* first published in 1899. The book, used by art teachers at Columbia Teachers' College for the next twenty years, was inspired by Dow's discovery of the new Post-Impressionist art and rediscovery of Oriental art. Dow's passionate appreciation for color grew out of his studies with Paul Gauguin at Pont Aven, France. Dow experimented with vivid complementary color juxtapositions under Gauguin's bold tutelage. O'Keeffe's lively color sense was thus finally encouraged.

Her lasting interest in Oriental art also began with Dow's book. In Boston, he had studied Japanese art and brushwork with the Orientalist Ernest Fenellosa. Dow was introduced to, and adopted, many time-honored characteristics and methods of Oriental artists, including the flat compositional methods, simplicity of form, repetition of form and line, the symbolic or ritual use of colors and shapes, and the variation of the size or format of a painting to fit the particular subject being painted.

Dow simplified these significant new—and old—techniques with charts, color wheels, tone graphs, and other models that illustrated basic color, tone, and spatial relationships. Although his book made dull reading, Dow's methods provided more freedom than those of Vanderpoel and Chase. A wider choice of subject and style was inherent in Dow's emphasis on color, shape, line, and space. His idea of "filling space in a beautiful way" appealed so completely to O'Keeffe that it soon became her motto as well.

The second major influence during O'Keeffe's transition into her new style was the Russian abstractionist Wassily Kandinsky. O'Keeffe first read his book *Concerning the Spiritual in Art* at Bement's suggestion. Kandinsky's book supplied some of the concepts behind Dow's methods. Dow noted Ernest Fenellosa's theory "that 'space art' may be called 'visual music,'"[16] while Kandinsky discussed particular correspondences between works of art and the music of Moussorgsky, Schönberg, Scriabin, Mozart, and Beethoven. He also discussed the psychological effects of color—blue as heavenly, yellow as earthy, red as fiery and exciting. He used a musical metaphor to express the role of color:

Generally speaking, color directly influences the soul. Color is the keyboard, the eyes are the hammers, the soul is the piano with many strings. The artist is the hand that plays, touching one or another purposively, to cause vibrations in the soul.[17]

Kandinsky theorized that each color has a spiritual vibration—artists must first discover their innermost feelings and necessities and then create forms and colors that capture these essences. Feelings were extensions of the artist's spirit and soul, as opposed to imitation of Old Masters and blind obeisance to scientific methods of composition. Kandinsky called simple compositions done in this spirit "melodic" and more complex compositions "symphonic."

Georgia O'Keeffe adopted the most concrete aspects of these theories—especially the advice about color and forms. She had enough formal training and personal character to realize that by

Tent Door at Night, *1913, watercolor, 19" x 24¾"*

"feelings" Kandinsky was not advocating what painter Marsden Hartley called "a vast confusion of emotional exuberance in the guise of [the] ecstatic fullness" that is "second-rate experience."[18] In Kandinsky's exuberant, individualized abstractions, his "feelings" were evident only in the immediacy and freshness of each design. As a teacher and artist, O'Keeffe relied on the theories of Dow and Kandinsky from 1913 until 1918, when she moved to New York. By that time she had incorporated some of their formal concerns into her art and arrived at her own style, which became archetypal and spare over the next fifty years. Painter John Marin, whose relation to nature is comparable to O'Keeffe's, noted:

Seems to me the true artist must perforce go from time to time to the elemental big forms—Sky, Sea, Mountain, Plain—and those things pertaining thereto, to sort of re-true himself up, to recharge the battery. For these big forms have everything. But to express these, you have to love these, to be a part of these in sympathy . . .[19]

This idealized view of nature had been the wellspring for the American transcendentalists. Although O'Keeffe never stated *her* love of "elemental big forms" in words, she did revere nature, and in the act of painting, if not in words, nature became the primary source and focus of her art.

Tent Door at Night, a watercolor done in 1913, is one of the earliest examples of O'Keeffe's new approach to art. Three curving triangles create a pup tent as seen from inside. An aqua-blue central triangle of sky is divided vertically by a narrow tent pole and dangling canvas tie at the tent opening. The sky is trisected into a top area of pale blue and two lower triangles of medium blue. An unpainted edge that separates the dark triangles of the tent from the sky imitates the effect of twilight and underscores the natural geometry of the shapes. These tonal relationships reverse the traditional use of a dark central form with lighter ground. The olive drab tent floor is depicted in an irregular lower triangle. The tent door and walls appear as quarter circles of cerulean blue whose circumferences curve away from each other

as the rest of the form is cut off by the rectangular edges of the canvas. The tent shapes are truncated circles as well as triangles, so the viewer, without realizing it, is enmeshed in the mixed, irregular complementaries of both circles and triangles. The tent image is so natural that its complex geometrical structure is not obvious. The image of dusk inside a tent remains the immediate and primary focus.

O'Keeffe's previous art credentials and her performance in Bement's advanced drawing class earned his respect, and he invited her to be his assistant the following summer. At the suggestion of a Chatham classmate from Texas, O'Keeffe had also applied for the position of drawing supervisor in the public school system in Amarillo, Texas. She was hired immediately. At the end of August 1912, O'Keeffe arrived by train in Amarillo, a cattle-shipping center which seemed, to her, a dot on the vast, arid, endless Texas plains.

For the next two years, O'Keeffe spent each school year teaching in Texas. She explored the flat plains and rocky canyons, returning each summer to her family and a summer position at the university. This move to a rugged western town, coupled with her first independence from family, art teachers, and peers, provided O'Keeffe with Wild West stories to match those her mother had told. She decided to stay at the Magnolia Hotel, a modest but lively establishment where she could go her own way, put an ear to the gossip of shootings and scandals in the frontier town, and keep her distance from the other teachers.

After accepting responsibility for the art education of the elementary students, O'Keeffe decided to use Dow's methods to show the children how to draw the objects around them. She encouraged the children to paint what they loved best. One day she even got them to help her hoist a child's long-haired pony onto her desktop so they could draw it.[20] Her supervisors may have heard about this incident; in any case, O'Keeffe's nontraditional approach was suspect. Her supervisors felt strongly that the state-approved textbook should be used by all students. Hadn't she begun her art education with copybooks? O'Keeffe refused to order the books. Her high spirits put her in a mood to buck the establishment. She put her past illnesses, the unstable health of both parents, and uncertainties about the future in the distance and grew as hardy as the stray desert plants she passed on long, long walks across the plains.

O'Keeffe's art had little in common with the New York art world. In 1913, Alfred Stieglitz exhibited his own photographs at 291 as a contrast to the modern art being shown at New York's 69th Regiment Armory. As Marcel Duchamps's *Nude Descending a Staircase* stunned critics at the Armory with its cubism, movement, and distortion, O'Keeffe's work, such as *Tent Door at Night,* remained as serene and contemplative as her life in Amarillo. She was closer to nature—the evening star, the endless dusty flats—than to works being shown in New York.

From the Plains, *1919, oil on canvas, 27⁷⁄₈″ x 23⁵⁄₈″*

2. Georgia O'Keeffe and Anita Pollitzer

The friendship between Georgia O'Keeffe and Anita Pollitzer began when both were studying art in New York in 1914. At Bement's suggestion, O'Keeffe was taking a course with Arthur Dow at Columbia University's Teachers' College. She also sat in on Charles Martin's class at the Art Students League, where she and two others, Dorothy True and Anita Pollitzer, drew still lifes while the rest of the students copied plaster casts.

At twenty-seven, O'Keeffe was older than most of the students, but she developed friendships with two classmates, Dorothy True, a voluptuous, sophisticated young woman from Maine, and Anita, a whirlwind of energy committed to new ideas in art and suffrage for women. The acquaintance developed into friendship as O'Keeffe and Pollitzer began a correspondence that lasted from 1915 until 1965—the longest recorded association that O'Keeffe ever maintained. The letters of 1915–1916 are more than the primary record of important stages of O'Keeffe's artistic growth. Anita provided the enthusiasm, the art news, and the entree to impresario/photographer Alfred Stieglitz that fueled O'Keeffe's drive to be an artist and led to her first gallery exhibition—her first public recognition as an artist.

Anita, the youngest daughter of Clara and Gustav Morris Pollitzer, grew up in Charleston, South Carolina. Clara was a former German teacher with a degree from Hunter College and Morris was a cotton exporter and civic activist. Anita could read, write, and play the piano before she entered grade school, and she had already taken a college art course in South Carolina before entering Teachers' College. The perky, energetic twenty-year-old was already involved in the new trends in music, art, and politics; she later became a national leader in the women's suffrage movement.

Anita and Dorothy True both visited Stieglitz at 291 with O'Keeffe. Dorothy later helped Stieglitz at 291 and posed for a classic photograph in 1919—an accidental double exposure created a provocative image depicting her face reflected on one leg in a high-heeled shoe. Anita visited 291 to discuss art and life with the philosophical Stieglitz. O'Keeffe, more shy than her two friends, remained at a safe distance to avoid Stieglitz's pointed and often personal manner of questioning visitors.

All too soon, O'Keeffe had to return to Charlottesville. As she began to teach the summer art session at the university, she laughed when she received a formal letter to "Miss O'Keefe" closing "from Anita L. Pollitzer." Two marvelous bits of art news prompted a quick response from O'Keeffe. The first was that Anita regretted that *The Life and Letters of Vincent Van Gogh* was out of print when she went to buy a copy at Brentano's, and the second was that, to end her disappointment, she had gone to 291 to visit Mr. Stieglitz. Anita wrote from her hometown in the South to O'Keeffe's:

(From Charleston, South Carolina, to Charlottesville, Virginia)
June 10, 1915

Dear Miss O'Keefe,
. . . I spent the weekend after I saw you in the country around New York. I came back on a Tuesday and flew up to Brentano's to get our "Life and Letters of Vincent Van Gogh", only to find much to my horror and sorrow that it has just gone out of print! They had another book there called "Personal Recollections of Vincent Van Gogh" which I glanced over, but it wouldn't have been particularly suitable for Mr. Martin. It simply talked about the man and the clothes he wore, what kind of canvas he bought, what he ate for breakfast & such things—so I wouldn't get it. I looked over all the other books & Art magazines & I didn't see any thing at all suitable—I felt like yelling to you to come back and pick out the thing—

Then I had a brilliant idea—I went to the Photo Secession and asked Mr. S. to show me some old numbers of Camera Work—He said "Why?" I said "I want to buy one"—He said—"Let me pick out the most wonderful one we have"—and it was an old Rodin number—the most exquisite thing you can possibly imagine—Oh I wish you might see it. It has four fine Steichen photographs in the

front. And then marvelous color reproductions of about 8 or 9 Rodin color drawings—Magnificent nudes with color touches in—So I bought it—It was three dollars but worth a million— . . . Mr. Stieglitz said—You can sell this Rodin no. for $25 whenever you want to—we haven't many more in print . . .

. . . so goodbye, love to you—don't teach too hard—and paint—from

Anita L. Pollitzer
who hopes you won't mind this scrawl [1]

The Rodin drawings were to influence O'Keeffe's nude series of 1917. This issue of *Camera Work* recalled her visit to see the Rodins at 291 with other League students. Unlike Rodin, O'Keeffe would be her own model. She now sent Anita advice, reading suggestions, and questions about books unavailable in Charlottesville. Anita advised O'Keeffe not to get stuck teaching if she could "do work for herself" and "make piles of money." Both statements were prophetic:

(Summer 1915)

Pat! Such a letter—It was perfectly great and so good to get it—you write letters exactly like yourself, and I love them! . . . Pat—perhaps you're right about my not going to the League, but I hate to risk not going there at least for a try—I think you rather forget that while Mr. Bement & people who let you stumble around may be good for you now, *they wouldn't have been before you'd had good solid grinding . . . Of course I'd a million times rather work any where—float around 291—the College Life Rooms, but I rather think I'd be sorry at the end of the year . . . I hate to think of your teaching those people how to draw red apples that aren't "absolutely round"—of course you might have extra time to do work for yourself—and you might make piles of money and come up north the year after . . . Oh—before I forget—Kandinsky's "Art of Spiritual Harmony"—is published by Houghton Mifflin Company—Boston & New York—It gets better with each rereading—I've really digested most of it—now—it's good . . . Your "Woman as World Builders" sounds very interesting. I've been doing Suffrage work on the side this summer—Just private conversions of course—I worked hard for it the week I was in Charleston—was one of a deputation to visit our Congressman— gave out Suffrage Literature and Lemonade at a booth & such things . . .*

Loads of Love
Anita

O'Keeffe replied in her large oval script punctuated with curving dashes. Bold, self-confident, and graceful as the handwriting appeared, O'Keeffe was still tentative about her art. She sent Anita a roll of drawings that she had done in less than an hour each, and wondered if they were "half done." The idea of art as music, as suggested in Kandinsky's book, must have been on her mind, for she was careful to note that she hadn't *listened* to music while drawing. Yet she called her art "music"—"my own tune."

Anita's eight-page reply contained more art news. She had loved Stieglitz's latest issue of *291*—with a cover by John Marin— and had asked Stieglitz to send her friend a copy.[2] Her critique of O'Keeffe's art was characteristically supportive and noncritical:

(From "Fernwood," Hendersonville, North Carolina, to University of Virginia, Charlottesville, Virginia)

July 26, 1915

The drawings were a gorgeous surprise . . . I have fixed up one of the rooms in our big old barn—as a kind of studio—& I took them up—thumb-tacked them on the walls & had a real exhibit. I was perfectly crazy about your small flower study, the one with the dark redish background—I think it's good! Your music was beautiful in color—I liked the blue & yellowish steps picture [sketch] ever so much, also the redish purplish brick building picture—the one in which the building went clear out to the top of the paper—(not the one with the tomb stone) You certainly have

done lots of work. My family came up several times to see your exhibit, & they were the only visitors I allowed. My sisters were in love with the poppies. I liked their big feeling & thought the color very lovely but I thought that your two lowest big poppies made rather a bad design. I thought one left out made it better— remember?

. . . Did you get a 291 number? . . . I loved my last month's one—the Marin cover so I ordered one for you from Mr. Stieglitz—I hope he had some left—and sent it . . . Are your big pupils learning lots—Leave them alone & go out & paint! Then send me some more.

Anita

O'Keeffe spent the summer working on her art, throwing out work which didn't satisfy her, reading *291* and *The Masses,* and socializing. She began seeing a young professor, Arthur Mac-Mahon, who was teaching government that summer at the university. Arthur, a New Yorker with liberal political ideas, had introduced her to books encouraging women's self-determination, such as Floyd Dell's *Women as World Builders,* which advocated that women pursue satisfying professional work alongside men rather than be ruled solely by their emotions. O'Keeffe took this advice literally and told Anita that Arthur was a perfect friend because they never got mushy. At twenty-eight, O'Keeffe still kept boyfriends at a safe distance, true to the class prophesy at Chatham.

That autumn 1915, Anita was again enrolled in the League and sent O'Keeffe art news from New York. O'Keeffe wanted to be in New York too, but she had been offered a teaching position in Columbia, South Carolina, at a Methodist junior college. As with her later moves, she worried about what she would miss, but decided at the last minute to accept the position. She also sent her friend Dorothy True more of her art to show to their teacher at the League, Mr. Martin.

Anita wrote often, noting that their teacher, Miss Cowell, had

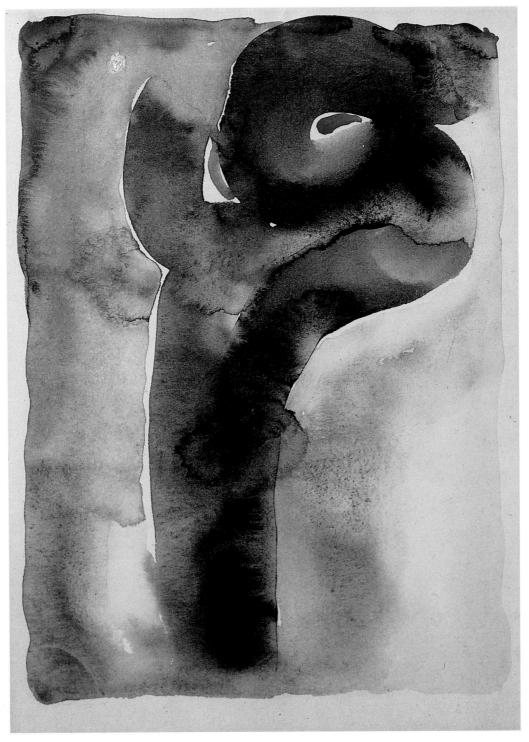

Portrait W—No. 1, *1917, watercolor, 12" x 9"*

Trees and Picket Fence, *1918, watercolor on paper, 18" x 12"*

a big surface design by O'Keeffe hanging in her studio—"it knocked me flat on my back, the moment I opened the door." Anita's letter of October 8 contained more news of Stieglitz:

. . . I hurried down to 291 and saw our friend Stieglitz. He's a great man pat, and it does me good to breathe his air for a little while. Nothing was on the walls—everything was on the floors— he was in the back room sneezing like a tornado when I entered—He came out when he got good and ready, and we talked like old times. Then he and I went in the back room and he gave me my "291" numbers—Isn't the Picasso violin one a beauty. Walkowitz was there too. I told Mr. Stieglitz I was going to the League and to my surprise—he said—"Do it"—Walkowitz then spoke up in his funny quiet little way and said—'You know what I think—that you should go to the league and learn all they've got to teach you—then work by yourself and forget all you can of what they've told you and what's left will be the part that's good for you." . . .

Pat I told him where you were and that I hated you to be there and he said "Say—don't tell me—I know" in that way of his and then he said—"When she gets her money—she'll do Art with it— and if she'll get anywhere—it's worth going to Hell to get there."

Until she received this word of Stieglitz from Anita, O'Keeffe's notes had been brief and morose. Becoming acclimated to the stuffy old Confederate city of Columbia, whose cotton-based economy was in tatters due to World War I, would be impossible. The Methodist college was in debt due to declining enrollment and a recent fire. The prevailing beliefs in religious and feminine virtues were stifling to O'Keeffe. After the move, she complained of feeling sick inside "as if I could dry up and blow away," of the bad taste that Thomas Hardy's *Return of the Native* gave her, and that her friend Arthur was "too nice to let go—and too nice to keep." She gave Anita a lecture on self-control that strongly underscored her own prerogatives. From her point of view, Anita was too susceptible to her feelings—she should save them and prac-

tice the control to remain clear, independent, and sane—and to keep going. Although she was steering clear of a major commitment in her relationship with Arthur, O'Keeffe accelerated her persistence and emotional involvement toward the works she was creating. She joked about a watercolor series on which she had been working for over a week: "Today's is the tenth edition of it—and there it stands saying—'Am just deliciously ugly and unbalanced'!"

O'Keeffe's mood changed dramatically after Anita's letter with advice from Stieglitz. As she read the letter on her way back from the post office, she dropped her other things and stood laughing. She regained her longstanding ability to distance herself from her immediate surroundings through her insular personality and began to work furiously on her art that very day. She had enough energy left to go for a long walk with eight schoolgirls, jogging so easily that none could keep up with her. After rereading the letter a third time, she wrote:

Anita—do you know—I believe I would rather have Stieglitz like something—anything I had done—than anyone else I know of—I have always thought that—if I ever make anything that satisfies me even ever so little—I am going to show it to him to find out if it's any good . . .[3]

Her next letter was even more expansive, and, subconsciously, quite romantic. The wonderful question—"Do you feel like flowers sometimes?"—expresses her own inner joy consummated in an identification with nature.

O'Keeffe had already developed a reserve that would not allow her to admit her feelings of joy, happiness, or love *explicitly* in words or behavior. It suited her to code her feelings in concrete terms. She had filled her room with flowers—red and pink cosmos, pink/lavender and red/lavender petunias, and zinnias—and described how Arthur had inspired certain artworks. O'Keeffe was drawing and painting over two hours daily, taking long walks, teaching, and hearing regularly from Arthur, who was teaching

Anita Pollitzer *in student days, c. 1919, photographer unknown*

elsewhere. Admitting that she had been falling in love with him, she concluded that Anita's and Dorothy's letters had given her the necessary push to get back to work on her art. This attitude implies that a personal relationship was not compatible with her goals as an artist.

O'Keeffe perceived a schism between what was permissible in art and in life due to the prevailing attitudes at the turn of the century. Her unmarried aunts Ollie and Lola were prime examples of women who had chosen careers instead of marriage. Little did she realize that within three years she would enjoy breaking society's rules for a personal relationship and for art!

To free her imagination from the confining mores of Columbia, she began to read plays—Synge's *Riders to the Sea,* Euripides' *The Trojan Women,* Chekhov's *The Sea Gull*—and she reread Kandinsky's book. Behind her absolute reserve, a keen-edged quest for romance and embracing encounters with nature had begun. O'Keeffe sent Anita a roll of her latest artworks.

Anita's responses were again exuberant. In addition to heartfelt commentary, she wrote that she planned to send two pieces to a competition at the Philadelphia Academy of Art:

New York—October 14—1915
Wednesday night.

Your letter came this morning Pat—I read it at breakfast and it made me quite hungry! Now Pat—Here's why I'm writing.

I saw them yesterday—and they made me feel—*I swear they did—They have emotions that sing out or holler as the case may be. I'm talking about your pastels—of course. They've all got feeling Pat—written in red right over them—no one could possibly get your definite meaning Pat—that is unless they knew you better than I believe anyone does know you—but the mood is there everytime. I'll tell you the ones that I sat longest in front of:—*

The crazy one—all lines & colors & angles—There is none other like it so you'll know the one I mean—it is so consistently full & confused & crazy that it pleased me tremendously. It struck me as a perfect expression of a mood!—That was why I liked it— not because it was pleasing or pretty for it's far from that—It screams like a maniac & runs around like a dog chasing his tail. Then the flower study which I liked so much this summer, gives me infinite joy—It is just a beautiful little thing & I do like beautiful things sometimes.—Your color in that orange & red ball one—is very strong & powerful—It doesn't mean just as much to me as that first—I guess it's more yours Pat & less anybody else's. The blue-purple mountain is exquisitely fine & rare. It expresses perfect strength—but a kind not a brutal strength.

Your trees—green & purple are very simple & stand well & firmly. I like that as it is—but Dorothy wrote you what Mr. Martin said, I guess, last night. Then the smaller one of the yellow & redish orange pictures struck me as awfully good but I didn't like it—It meant something awfully different to me & I couldn't get that out of my head. Your monotype that you did of me is a masterpiece! I think anyone could have done those Hollyhocks but Mr. Martin seemed to think they should be sent to Philadelphia & the mono- type too of course. Pat I wrote for entry cards for the Philadelphia Water Club tonight & we're going to fill two out for you for the Hollyhocks & monotype. I sent them an envelope addressed to you & told them to send you two entry cards (in case you spoil one). If you've decided to fix your big simple trees—frame it & send it— then make out an entry card for it as soon as you get it. Send it to (The Pennsylvania Art Academy/Broad & Arch Streets/Phil. Penn.) Remember Dorothy will make out the cards for these that she's sending—so unless you send the trees or something—don't make out cards. Send the stuff right away tho—if you're going to . . .

I'm going to the little Bandbox theatre this Saturday night to see 4 good Modern Plays—written & acted by the Masses crowd [radical activists based in Greenwich Village] & Washington Square people—stunning

staging they say—
good night Pat—

Anita

O'Keeffe was not only taking herself more seriously as an art- ist—she was now questioning the very meaning of art. Anita couldn't supply that answer, but she was able to articulate, in her own way, the notion of "source" that they had learned from Dow and Kandinsky:

October 26, 1915

. . . went autoing 2–7 yesterday—out past Yonkers & Rye & Has- tings—all along the Hudson. It was wondrously cool and the golds & oranges & yellows were stunning! The reflection of those colors each one mad to be the brightest—and the palisades all violet & dark reds & blues was really worth while. There's an awful lot that is worth while Pat—really—isn't there . . .

Pat—you're screamingly funny—I shook absolutely when I came to the serious part of your letter asking me what Art is—Do you think I know what art is? Do you think I'd think anybody knew, even if they said they did? Do you think I'd care what any- body thought? Now if you ask me what we're trying to do that's a different thing—We're trying to live (& perhaps help other people to live) by saying or feeling—things or people—on canvas or pa- per—in lines, spaces & color. At least I'm doing that—Matisse per- haps cares chiefly for color—Picabia for shapes—Walkowitz for line—perhaps I'm wrong—but I should care only for those things in so far as they helped me express my feeling—To me that's the end always—To live on paper what we're living in our hearts & heads; & all the exquisite lines & good spaces & rippingly good colors are only a way of getting rid of these feelings & making them tangible— . . .

Throughout the fall and winter, their letters showed their growth and appreciation of each other's different worlds. Both women played piano and O'Keeffe was now practicing away on the violin. Anita had the advantage of going to concerts at Carne- gie Hall, art exhibitions, and inspiring lectures by artists such as George Bellows, all of which she reported to her friend. She

Chicken in Sunrise, *1917, watercolor on paper, 11¹⁵/₁₆" x 8¹³/₁₆"*

enjoyed describing New York's cultural highlights—"Kreisler played a Brahms Sonata that was bigger than any word in the Language we speak." She talked of Van Gogh and then Picasso exhibitions at the Modern Gallery; conversations with Stieglitz's associates, artists Walkowitz and Zorach; art tips, news; and the adorable boys in the art class she was teaching at Horace Mann Elementary School. Now that Anita was engaged in adult responsibilities and close to receiving her degree from Teachers' College at Columbia, she treasured her friendship with O'Keeffe more than ever. O'Keeffe noted in November how much she loved hearing about Bellows; she apologized for not being able to write about things. So she sent art that Anita received on November 16. Anita replied the same day with comments and the wish that she could show them to Stieglitz—"I don't feel the time's come yet—but keep on working this way like the devil."

As O'Keeffe pursued her own course, trying to answer her own question, "What is Art anyway?" her letters began to glow. She cultivated her sense of being different from the other teachers, telling Anita she wished the Methodist faculty would go to hell, perhaps echoing Stieglitz's use of the word in advice sent via Anita. Georgia took long walks in the woods, and spent many hours in her little studio next to the art room and in her room, where fresh flowers and numbers of *291* tacked on the wall gave a corner of the room a special feeling. O'Keeffe's letters were becoming shorter. Her friend Arthur had surprised her with a Thanksgiving visit. The wonderful time they had stunned her and left a funny feeling now that he was gone. After his visit, O'Keeffe's new series of abstractions, done exclusively in charcoals, were big with feelings she had to express.

Three of these early works show O'Keeffe's flat handling of perspective and design and offer a preview of the forms that became her trademark. *Special Number 14* presents a one-dimensional view of three planes and shapes. The bottom portion and first plane of the drawing is a globe with snaking curves of light. Although O'Keeffe had never been in an airplane, which was the

Coxcomb, *date unknown, oil on canvas, 20½" x 17½"*

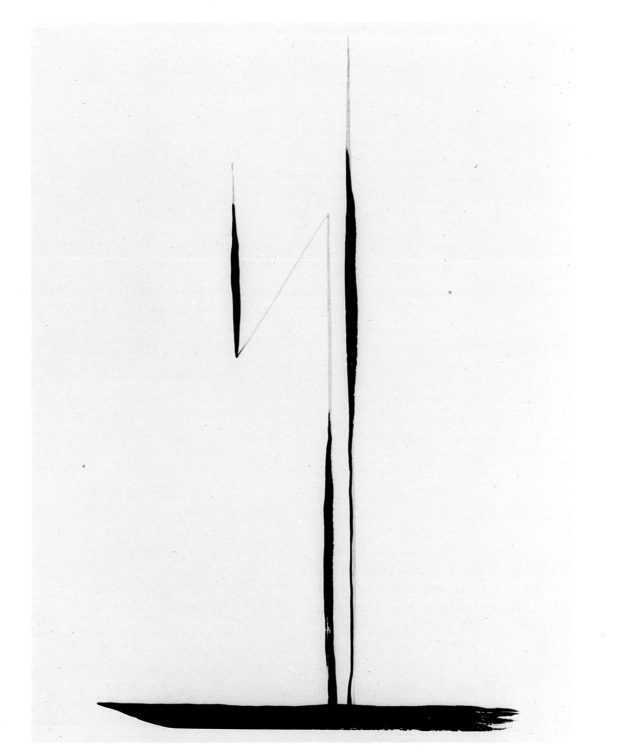

Black Lines, *1916, watercolor, 24½" x 18½"*

Morning Glory with Black, *1926, oil on canvas, 35^{13}/$_{16}$" x 39^{5}/$_{8}$"*

White Flower, 1929, oil on canvas, 30⅛″ x 36⅛″

In the meantime, Georgia O'Keeffe had an idea—that she could communicate her feelings directly in lines and rhythms. By finding the "cutting edge" of each line and movement, O'Keeffe eventually achieved the flow and unified simplicity she sought. In late January, as she curled up in her room to read a letter from Stieglitz, she soon decided to create more works using her new idea. By February, she had more work to send to Stieglitz—as soon as she could locate a roll for mailing. When the Canyon, Texas, administrators wanted her to agree to take "Pa" Dow's methods class that summer, she kicked up her heels and decided to take it that spring.

O'Keeffe's old-fashioned looks were a direct contrast with her avant-garde attitude toward art. By this time in her life, her conservative mode of dressing noted by Chatham classmates was even more pronounced. She had adopted a patrician style, wearing only black—a classic dress with a square white collar, with her hair drawn back tightly into a bun. She enjoyed the severity of her looks—the opposite of the style of women in Columbia.

She may have dressed in black, but O'Keeffe's heart was filled with spring colors. She was rereading issues of *The Masses* and *291*—and she tacked the one with the Marin cover to her brown wood bureau. Marin's fine etching of the Woolworth Building, "flying around, falling down," as she described it to Anita, pointed to an exciting direction, and to Manhattan!

As she prepared to leave Columbia, O'Keeffe's grim mood vanished, and she had a final party, inviting friends to visit her room all night long, whispering first by candlelight, then in the dark. She even decided to show art professor Hill her work for the first time. As she expected, he laughed and called her drawings mad. Then, with mixed feelings of agony and glee, she gave the local art club a lecture about modern art—her way of saying goodbye, or "wake up!" to the dull town. Ever protective of her works, she cautioned Anita not to show works she had sent to Bement and others.

Spring semester at Columbia Teachers' College in New York was just about over when O'Keeffe was told that "Virginia O'Keeffe" was in a group exhibition at 291. No one was there the first time she visited—Stieglitz was on jury duty. She looked at her works, slowly, and left. The next week, O'Keeffe found Stieglitz alone at the gallery. She requested that he take her art down, but he talked her into leaving it up. Her protest to the great impresario that the exhibition was unauthorized is already part of the O'Keeffe legend. The real mystery is *who* supplied Stieglitz with those works? Had she sent the roll herself? Was she really too shy to show them in public or just annoyed that she hadn't been consulted?

The legend concerning the first exhibition has been recounted by Herbert J. Seligmann, a poet and critic who was close to Stieglitz:

Whatever of life and vital impulse came to America, or out of America, was fatally and inevitably attracted to the small exhibition rooms and the burning spirit that centered there. So it was that drawings sent from Texas by a young woman to a friend in New York, with the injunction to show them to no one, came to Stieglitz because the friend felt he must see them. "Finally, a woman on paper," Stieglitz exclaimed, recognizing at once their profound significance. In this way, after he had examined the drawings daily for months, and shown them to many sensitive people, to make sure they really contained what he felt was there, came about the first exhibition of Georgia O'Keeffe. [6]

This account is typical of succeeding versions in its emphasis on fate and on Stieglitz's "woman on paper" remark. The rapport that already existed between Pollitzer and Stieglitz and the fact that Pollitzer received many sets of drawings before she decided to show a set to Stieglitz, as well as O'Keeffe's statement to Pollitzer that she would value Stieglitz's approval above all others, are realities that underlie the myth.

That summer, teaching art at the University of Virginia, O'Keeffe

Red and Blue Plums, *1920, oil on canvas, 9" x 12"*

looked forward to notes from Stieglitz. He wrote that her draw-ings had attracted attention and interest and continued to bring him pleasure, and that he looked forward to new works. He noted that the future was "hazy," without mentioning that the streets were filled with soldiers. A "world thinking war" was only one of the dilemmas Stieglitz did not mention.[7] O'Keeffe was listless; she would typically spend the mornings teaching, the afternoons sleeping, and the evenings working. The cool, rainy weather was dreary. At night the impressive colonial façades of the campus were newly lit and serene.

O'Keeffe responded only once to Anita's flurry of summer let-ters. Her self-confidence as an artist was growing, and her com-munications with Stieglitz had become primary. He had sent her five issues of *Camera Work* and a book, *The Man of Promise,* which she intended to read soon. O'Keeffe stayed up almost a whole night creating a plasticene sculpture of a curved, rising

Evening Star III, *1917, watercolor, 9″ x 11⅞″*

shape. Did she realize that it resembled an erect penis? The rising shaft was abstract, yet the phallic image was obvious, even to viewers unaware that Freud's analyses of subconscious influences were sweeping intellectual circles in America and Europe. O'Keeffe made a plaster mold and two plaster copies. Anita heard about the piece, but O'Keeffe never told her what the shape was, or meant. The artifact, boldly containing a sexuality she had rarely shown in real life, was her secret gift to Stieglitz. The art tapped unconscious forces which O'Keeffe, due to her stern rural upbringing and silent reserve, would *never* name.

Stieglitz, who was fifty-two in 1916, was already prone to numerous ailments. He now expressed his concern about O'Keeffe's health. He also sent photographs of her exhibition, which she admired and appreciated greatly. O'Keeffe wrote on July 27 that he could do as he pleased with her art—that "they are as much yours as mine."[8] This note marked a major change in her attitude toward Stieglitz. She realized that he cherished her letters and art. In fact, Stieglitz's habit of reverently carrying the art around with him became something of a joke to his cronies.

That summer O'Keeffe's mother died. She made little mention of the fact. Although obedient to her mother's demands and expectations, O'Keeffe had never been able to confide in her. Her father was still alive, but his presence was even more remote; there is no record of any further communications between O'Keeffe and her father except for a mention of his death in November 1918.[9] O'Keeffe somehow detached her life from her parents long before they went their own ways. In contrast, the communications with Stieglitz offered both a closeness and confidentiality that neither had ever experienced. Anita, knowing each better than they yet knew each other, explained it this way:

Their letters undoubtedly brought them closer than a person so withdrawing as Georgia would have allowed in conversation. To say that she understood Stieglitz would be an exaggeration. But that was not important to him, for he did not expect to be "under-stood." But from the outset of their correspondence, each filled an amazing need in the other's life. The artist in Georgia went out to the artist in Stieglitz.[10]

O'Keeffe sent some drawings to Stieglitz in late August. On her way to her new teaching job in Canyon, Texas, she went camping with a friend and his wife. They traveled from Charlottesville to Knoxville to Natural Bridge together. In Asheville, O'Keeffe went off with another friend, Katherine, to Weaversville and Beach Mountain, North Carolina. She then took a train to Canyon for the opening of the school year. She told Anita that her last letter was stingy compared to the big one she had needed and received from Stieglitz.

Canyon was much smaller than Amarillo. She compared the lowing of the cattle to music—a tune that fit into her world of ground and sky. The elements, especially the evening sky and a nearby canyon, were visually and spiritually exhilarating. On long walks in the evenings and early mornings, O'Keeffe watched zigzags of lightning electrify the oceanlike expanse of land and sky and listened to the wind. She began to paint the sky—its changing colors, the evening star, and the moon as it seemed to rise directly from the flat horizon. The Evening Star Series began as a simple design of sky with a curling void in the center resembling a broad question mark on its side. In successive works, the tail and circles within the void were delineated in broad bands of colors, such as red, orange, and yellow. The colors, representing light waves, were separated from each other by thin unpainted edges. The evening star was a small unpainted void in the center from which light was (implicitly) emanating. The successive stages of this series show the thought and time—over a year—that O'Keeffe took, even during this period, to develop an idea.[11]

West Texas State Normal College was a new building, completed that April after a fire had destroyed the old building. Despairing that there were only a handful of art books, Georgia sent Anita ten dollars and requested photos of textiles, Greek pottery,

Persian plates, and anything else that she could show to her design students. She was teaching costume design and interior decoration.

O'Keeffe had moved from her first rented room, which was too pink—pink roses with gold tails on the wallpaper and pink roses on the two rugs—to an unadorned room on the other, rougher side of town. One September night, she watched a tremendous thunderstorm with another roomer, a big old workingman. As the storm raged, flared, and died down, she spent the rest of the night reading and rereading Longfellow's translation of *The Divine Comedy.*

Anita sent her the requested photographs and a book list from Brentano's recommending Huntington Wright and Clive Bell. O'Keeffe wrote back that Stieglitz had sent nine photographs of her exhibition. She eventually sent these to Anita, noting that in spite of mixed feelings about her art, the photographs of the pieces were especially fine.

O'Keeffe totally immersed herself in preparations for her art classes. She was reading Sir William Petrie's book *The Arts and Crafts of Ancient Egypt,* Charlotte Perkins Gilman's "The Dress of Women" in a 1915 volume of *The Forerunner,* Wright's *Creative Will,* and Clive Bell's new book *Art.*[12] Bell's style reminded O'Keeffe of Alon Bement's, but Bell had more pep. Stieglitz had sent her Bayard Taylor's translation of *Dr. Faustus,* which she connected to vague recollections of reading Faust at age nineteen when she was quite ill. As busy as she was, O'Keeffe was making a new series of watercolors—gentle abstractions of nature that contained contrapuntal movements, a series simply titled Blue No. I (1916), Blue No. II (1916), etc. The keen-edged directness and striking simplicity of these works were noted by Anita:

September 27—1916

I'm sitting on the brown carpet again Pat—tonight with your three around me—three that I've picked out to like—because I love them—infinitely more than all the rest put together—They're very fine—two are very fine—and the cucumber is just truth—It's a fact—that's all—well said at that—but the other two are better than the truth! I'm glad blue is your color—I wonder if it is still— When did you do these three? But hang it—I haven't told you which three and I can't—How in the deuce would you describe such stuff—Never mind here you are—The pod of stuff standing quite erect & without assistance—near the other shape—is the one I called cucumber. It's rather self evident in meaning—I've known it always—but as art—(Dow's darned art) it's O.K.—very good—That's one of the three—and I like it—

This [sketch of Blue No. II (1916), watercolor] is very beautiful—Where did you keep the rest of yourself while you were doing it? Right's right—I wouldn't like one line different—There are dozens almost like it in this bunch—I wonder if this came first or last—The other ones most like it can't begin to touch it—I know you don't know what I'm talking about—Why aren't you here—! I shall keep that a while—on my wall—The other thing sitting near me is your [sketch of Blue No. I (1916), watercolor] tree-mountain-live forms in grey grey blue- & white—I shall also see how that is to live with. I've looked over all—& keep coming back to these—They mean much to me. & so different from your 291 others—Pat & yet the same— . . . I want to see Stieglitz . . .

. . night . . . Love
Anita

Since her sister Claudia was coming to visit, O'Keeffe needed to find a place where they could both live. She chose a newly built house on the edge of town, the residence of Dr. Douglas Shirley, a physics professor. O'Keeffe approached his wife, Willena, and asked to rent a room. Her daughter Louise recalls what happened next:

I was a child, just arrived, when Georgia was there. My mother was about the same age as Georgia. Our house had just been built, and my mother didn't want to rent a room, but Georgia

Pink Roses, *1934, pastel, 11¹³⁄₁₆″ x 7¹¹⁄₁₆″*

Sept. 27-1916   1.

I'm sitting on the brown carpet again Pat
tonight with your 3 around me — 3 that
I've picked out to like — because I love
them — infinitely more than all the rest put
together — They're very fine — 2 are very fine
— & the cucumber is just truth — Its a fact
Thats all — well said at that — but the
other two are better than the truth! I'm
glad blue is your color — I wonder if it
is still — where did you do these 3?
Don't hang it — I haven't told you
which 3 + I can't — How in the
fence would you describe such stuff
Nevermind here you are — The part of
stuff standing quite erect + without
assistance — near the other shape —
is the one I called cucumber. Its rather
self evident in meaning — I've known it
always — but as art — (Dow's darned
art) its O.K. very good — Thats one
of the 3 — I like it —

2.

This [sketch] is very beautiful —
Where did you keep
the rest of yourself
while you were
doing it?
Its right —

I wouldn't like one line different —
There are dozens almost like it
in this Punch — I wonder if this
came first or last — The other
ones not like it can't begin to touch it
I know you don't know what I'm talking
about — why ain't you here —
I shall keep that a while —
on my wall —
The other thing sitting near me is
your [sketch] tree — not — line forms
in grey grey blue — +
white — I shall
also see how that
is to live with.

3.

I've looked over all + keep coming back
to these — They mean much to me
+ so different from your others Pat — I
get the same —
                Next may I tell
you of the tiny little emeralds and
cobalt hill side + trees — Its so restful
I have to laugh — honestly I think
it's got a dandy mood, Nothing to
it — it won't last but my 3 will —
I hope to heaven you can remember
the ones I'm talking about — but I
bet you can't — This is no 4.

[sketch]

— I've just come back from a
glorious place in Greenwich Conn —
Very gay + giddy — + fun.
I'm to stay in New York till Dr. Mayor
says go + in the mean time
I'll work mornings with Miller
(Kenneth) + I aft with Mr. Martin
I'm neither glad nor sorry — but it's
got me — + I ought to see stuff
I couldn't write. Aline comes tomorrow. Keep
right on addressing me 51 East 60.
Oh I got the 10 pat — cashed it
+ very soon I'll be glad to get
good pictures for you — If you give
me time I'll write for dandies
from Boston. Write me if you can
wait a few weeks — It will
be good fun + practise. I spent
a morning with Alaskan Alon.
He's improved — asked for you — I couldn't
tell him much. Love Anita

Letter from Anita Pollitzer to Georgia O'Keeffe, September 27, 1916

insisted. It was a gabled upstairs room with no furniture, just an iron bed and a wood crate for supplies. She used to draw on the floor with her back to the closet door.

O'Keeffe was not friendly with the family and didn't eat here. Claudia was here part of the time. Georgia wanted the house because of the view from her window of the plains. But she was in her "black" period—she covered the windows with black and also wanted to paint over the natural wood baseboard—but mother said no. O'Keeffe was so different from everyone else that she was talked about. It was a small town. She didn't have many friends. She was an artist. She used to go to the canyon a lot. People still talk about Georgia. She was as different as they come.[13]

O'Keeffe kept to herself in Canyon—as she had in the other small towns where she had lived. Claudia arrived by January 1917. That month, O'Keeffe gave a Faculty Circle lecture on modern art, discussing aesthetics, Wright, Bell, Mexican caricaturist Marius de Zayas, critic Charles Henry Caffin, and Arthur Jerome Eddy. Although these critics, and their ideas, seemed ludicrous to some, O'Keeffe managed to involve the faculty members in a stimulating discussion that, to her intense satisfaction, crowded out another scheduled presentation.

She may have seemed odd to adults, but not to the high-school senior in charge of lighting the school play. He used to go for long walks with O'Keeffe until he was warned that he wouldn't graduate if his behavior continued. He obeyed the order, explaining the friendship only years later, "Did you ever see the rain with Georgia? Did you ever see her watch a great storm? I knew and loved that country well and here, for the first time, was someone who felt the same way about it. There was never anyone in the world like her in her appreciation of such things."[14]

When Anita saw Stieglitz that winter, she brought three of O'Keeffe's works. To her surprise, Stieglitz had an O'Keeffe on the gallery wall:

(From Charleston, South Carolina, to Canyon, Texas)

December 21, 1916

I'm back— . . . spent Saturday in Philadelphia at Fine Arts Academy with Dorothy, then took train . . . sent you back the photographs of yourself— . . . Pat take care of those things—& I sent you the drawings after giving him three to look at. He was wonderful—more than ever—but so much older—He gave me a Camera Work *and wrote such a wonderful thing in it—Make believe I haven't said it—I didn't go down before I left—I painted a lot before I left—things I wanted—I almost wanted him to see them—I did—but I couldn't. He asked me more than once. I had some visits that were marvellous! I never knew such a force—*

Your [sketch by Anita of Blue Lines *(1916), watercolor] only it's So fine—your two dependent on each other yet perfectly separate individual lines on fine dark blue—are on the wall—nearest to his back room. I was thunderstruck! What are you putting on paper now . . .*

O'Keeffe wrote to Anita that she had painted "slits in nothingness" where the canyon began. From the towering sandstone façade of the multihued, craggy cliffs, O'Keeffe had distilled the night-blackened slits of sky shooting like arrows between the stonefaces. This was the source of the two blue lines that Anita found in Stieglitz's gallery.

Blue Lines reveals O'Keeffe's new power. As both lines rise from a dark blue oval in the lower right center, each line has a mercurial, viscous quality, created by the two blues within each line. The controlled tension between the lines moves in another direction in the slivers of triangles shooting up at the tips. The lines also contrast cleanly with the unpainted ground and the lower oval of color. Mastery of line, indeed, was the key to O'Keeffe's question, "What is art anyway?" As nature was supplying models that no one else had noticed, her correspondence with Stieglitz was supplying great encouragement.

White Camelia, *1938, oil on canvas, 20⅝″ x 27⅜″*

3. Alfred Stieglitz and Georgia O'Keeffe

O'Keeffe moved to New York in 1918 at the invitation of Alfred Stieglitz. The period between her first solo exhibition at 291 in 1917 and her arrival in New York was strange even by her unorthodox standards. Teaching in Canyon, O'Keeffe ran into the same problems she had encountered in Amarillo: bucking the establishment. Her standoffish ways, her nonconformist teaching methods, and her refusal to support the war effort and show any patriotism contributed to an increasing mutual distrust between herself and the citizens of the small rural community.

Neither O'Keeffe nor her favorite correspondent Stieglitz sympathized with the war effort. Stieglitz, sympathetic to the Germans since his student days in Berlin, respected the German culture and remained loyal to individual friends. He felt that if President Woodrow Wilson had withheld arms and supplies from both sides, many lives would have been saved.[1] O'Keeffe's apolitical stand was, to some extent, modeled after Stieglitz's. Her character rebelled against war in general, and she, like Stieglitz, would never endorse military action for any reason.

When O'Keeffe took a leave of absence from teaching in February 1918 and moved into a farmhouse with her friend Leah Harris in Waring, Texas, near San Antonio, the stated reason for the leave was illness. No record of O'Keeffe's hospitalization exists, but her friend Leah was recovering from tuberculosis. O'Keeffe was well enough to take care of her friend, and her own leave probably stemmed from her strained relations with the community rather than the influenza epidemic. She had been isolated in Columbia, South Carolina, and in Amarillo, but Canyon was so small that her situation had become intolerable. O'Keeffe's spirits were definitely low, and she was not feeling healthy.

Stieglitz wanted to assess her actual situation and was alarmed at the possibility that O'Keeffe was unwell; over a half million Americans died of the flu in 1918. O'Keeffe was clearly discontented with her role as a teacher in a small town. Her two exhibitions under Stieglitz's sponsorship had given her the first taste of public recognition as an artist, and she yearned to be as free as the evening star—to be a star. Stieglitz realized O'Keeffe would need assistance if she decided to come to New York. Since he never traveled far himself, he sent photographer Paul Strand, his young protégé, to Texas by train to report on her health and help bring her east if she decided to come.

Stieglitz nervously inquired about O'Keeffe's health and art, recognizing her insecurity without a job or income. Strand's letters from Waring, Texas, to Stieglitz in New York included tales that resemble a soap opera scenario. He thought O'Keeffe was losing some of her vitality in her role of caring for Leah, and that she was leaning toward going to New York. In the meantime, a Dutch neighbor had insulted O'Keeffe and Leah, so Strand stepped in to even the score. He purchased a gun, invaded the neighbor's property, and confronted him, causing the terrified neighbor to press charges. The women had pressed charges as well; the sheriff was called in. Finally, the antagonist apologized for the slanderous statements he had made. Both sides finally dropped the charges against each other. Strand, careful not to elucidate lurid details, closed his long retelling of O'Keeffe's most recent confrontation with the locals with a description of O'Keeffe intensively painting a portrait of a local handyman, Brack, and with Leah's prophetic comment about O'Keeffe's future:

Today Georgia is feeling sick to her stomach but has been painting a picture of Brack all day—He is a strong fellow and very amusing—Has arms like that plumber you photographed—Sybl and Lucy may come out today—So we will be a crowd. Brack goes back tomorrow—Rest of us probably on Friday—Then I don't know—Leah said a few minutes ago that G was going to New York—that she wants to see her go—but feels somehow that she will come back South—Telegraph me if you feel that I am not doing anything or am doing something that you think might be done or left undone—Greetings—

[May 29, 1918][2]

Strand agreed with Leah that New York might be better for O'Keeffe now, but that the open spaces of the Southwest were better suited to her temperament.

Shortly thereafter, on June 10, Strand and O'Keeffe arrived at Pennsylvania Station. Stieglitz met them and took O'Keeffe to his niece Elizabeth's studio at 114 East 59th Street. Stieglitz's letters indicate that O'Keeffe had a cough and a cold when she arrived in New York, and he took her to see his brother Leopold, a doctor, when she was well enough to go out.

Their new relationship began in Elizabeth's studio. At first it was platonic; both respected his continuing, if disintegrating, home life with his wife Emmy. Their daughter Kitty was away at college. However, the mutual love Stieglitz and O'Keeffe shared for the arts and the strong bond created by their letters had set the stage for further closeness. He scheduled his daily visits to suit her painting hours and reported to his friends that she was producing "wonders." Curiously, few of these works have survived. Only three watercolors of 1918 were ever exhibited. Two were studies of outdoors subjects, *The Flag* and *Trees and Picket Fence,* which seem to be impressions of Lake George done a few months later. One was an addition to The Nude Series of eleven watercolors done in 1917. From Leah's, O'Keeffe had sent Stieglitz a roll of watercolors and drawings, including the nudes.

Stieglitz kept his cameras at his apartment and 291, so the idea of photographing O'Keeffe involved her active cooperation. One day, about a month after her arrival, he invited her to a photo session at his apartment. His wife, Emmy, who had been out shopping, returned earlier than expected; she immediately went into a rage, driving the two out of the house. That night she gave her husband an ultimatum: stop seeing O'Keeffe or move out.

Emmeline Obermeyer Stieglitz was the sister of Joseph Qbermeyer, Stieglitz's roommate in Germany and later partner (with their other roommate Louis Schubart) in his only business venture, the Photochrome Engraving Company. Emmy had married Stieglitz in high style at Sherry's, a stylish restaurant/ballroom, in

Birch Trees at Dawn at Lake George, *1926, oil on canvas, 36" x 30"*

Lake George Blue, *1926, oil on canvas, 18″ x 30″*

Lake George, *1923, oil on canvas, 18" x 32¼"*

Georgia O'Keeffe *by Alfred Stieglitz, 1918, photograph*

1893. Stieglitz and his twenty-year-old bride had boarded the S.S. *Bourgogne* for a honeymoon in Europe; upon their return, their first residence had been the Savoy Hotel. Both had come from upper-middle-class mercantile families of German-Jewish heritage. To Stieglitz, as to his father, Judaism meant little or nothing. His religion was belief in the human spirit.

The marriage had lasted over twenty-five years, notwithstanding Emmy's lack of interest in her husband's deepest artistic goals. She was involved with social events, travel, and fashions. She was light-headed and self-centered, and their life-styles were impossible to reconcile, leading to innumerable arguments. Emmy's extravagance was supported in part by her family and in part by an annual three-thousand-dollar stipend from Stieglitz's father, but money was a constant source of tension. With help from her brothers, Emmy made the primary purchases for their apartment at 1111 Madison Avenue, into which they moved in September 1898, just before the birth of their daughter, Katherine. Kitty grew up with a nurse, then a governess. Stieglitz's strained relations with his wife hampered his ability to get to know his only daughter.

As a meaningful alternative to his uneasy home life, Stieglitz had immersed himself in his pursuit of excellence in photography. He was zealous and independent about the format and editorial policy of the now celebrated publications *Camera Notes* (1897–1902) and *Camera Work* (1902–1917). He fought the more conservative members of the Camera Club to produce the former and produced the latter periodical independently. He pushed himself so hard that he came down with pneumonia in 1895 and suffered from exhaustion in 1898 and 1902. Health was important to Stieglitz, and it became a factor in his concern for O'Keeffe. Just as he sent daily letters to Emmy whenever she was away, he had been sending daily messages to O'Keeffe in Texas.

Casting aside the carefully maintained fiction of his marriage, Stieglitz took his cue from Emmy's ultimatum and moved out at once. This unforeseen but not unwelcome event created an immediate intimacy in the two-room studio he now shared with O'Keeffe.[3] She painted near the skylight, where he often photographed her posed against one of her paintings. At certain hours of the day—when the light was best—she found herself in the eyes of Stieglitz and his camera. Stieglitz would dictate a pose before one of her paintings or the bare window, closing down the lens as far as possible to sharpen the image. During the long exposures that this process required, O'Keeffe was a patient model. Sixty years later, in her introduction to Stieglitz's book *Georgia O'Keeffe,* she finally admitted that sexual chemistry was involved in the making of these prints.[4]

Their unannounced relationship was soon evident to the artists in Stieglitz's immediate circle. He introduced O'Keeffe to Marin and Dove, two artists whose works reprinted in *291* had provided inspiration when she was in Columbia, South Carolina. She met his niece Elizabeth Stieglitz (whose studio they now occupied) and her forty-year-old friend Donald Davidson, whose increasing intimacy Stieglitz encouraged despite the reservations of other relatives. He wrote to friends that O'Keeffe's presence was intense, spontaneous, and uncommonly beautiful.[5]

O'Keeffe's life was changing rapidly. Stieglitz's love and attention, his interests and friendships totally replaced her spartan life in Texas. His large, ubiquitous family had already heard about O'Keeffe. Most of the family were not especially fond of Emmy, who stopped visiting the Stieglitz clan's summer house at Lake George after 1908. Kitty was still a regular summer visitor.

Fully aware of the highly charged situation, Stieglitz's mother, Hedwig, invited her son to bring O'Keeffe to Lake George less than two months after her arrival in New York. On August 1, 1918, Hedwig assertively welcomed the artist to the Stieglitz family's summer quarters. Surprised relatives studied the new boyish charm of Stieglitz. His renewed enthusiasm for the outdoors made him a leader on hikes, and he took O'Keeffe rowing each evening after dinner. His grandniece Sue Davidson Lowe has noted in her book *Stieglitz: A Memoir/Biography,* that the two

would hold hands until often, "their holding hands on the porch led them . . . to more intricate convolutions and suddenly to a mad dash into the house. In my day, seven years later, an occasional exchange of winks could trigger Georgia's blouse-unbuttoning sprint up the stairs and Alfred's laughing pursuit."[6]

"Hedwig's delight in her son's new romance, and the various reactions of his siblings, were on a relatively superficial level," according to Lowe. "To his daughter, Kitty, however, the situation was calamitous. Finding O'Keeffe still at her grandmother's home when she herself arrived for part of her vacation, Kitty created a storm severe enough to drive her father and his lover back to New York," Lowe noted. Kitty, a sophomore at Smith College, was deeply hurt by Stieglitz's relationship with O'Keeffe, and his open rejection of her mother affected her as well. This led to "the end of what had always been a rather tenuous father-daughter relationship," Lowe has concluded.[7]

The Stieglitz family's summers in rented cottages at Lake George had begun in the 1870s. During the early 1880s, the whole family lived and traveled in Europe, returning to New York and purchasing Oaklawn, their Lake George summer house, in 1886.

Stieglitz began his studies in Berlin in 1882, changing his course of study from engineering to photochemistry, with Professor Hermann Vogel, at the Berliner Technische Hochschule. His career as a photographer began in Europe; as he won numerous medals at competitions and exhibitions in England, Germany, and Italy, he gained widespread recognition as a fine photographer. By the time he moved back to New York City in 1890, his proven accomplishments in the art of photography put him ahead of photography enthusiasts in America, most of whom still pursued it as a hobby.

Stieglitz's father, Edward, a retired woolens merchant and amateur artist, and mother, Hedwig, both encouraged the idealistic talk and goals of their oldest son. Edward had given Alfred a three-thousand-dollar annual stipend since 1882, even though he himself returned to work for a few months in 1893. Stieglitz's three

White Trumpet Flower, *1932, oil on canvas, 30" x 40"*

Red Canna, *c. 1923, oil on canvas mounted on masonite, 36" x 29⅞"*

magazine and countless articles and reviews. At the same time, O'Keeffe controlled what went into these articles and never divulged anything personal, establishing a mystique that made the public more curious than ever. O'Keeffe was photographed by Ansel Adams, Philippe Halsman, Yousuf Karsh, and a younger generation of photographers, including William Clift and Victor Lobl. Art lovers in almost every decade were thus freshly acquainted with the ongoing portrait of O'Keeffe, and her classic features were often on view. Her sensitive hands cradle bone in 1930 as she cradles rock and sculpted clay forms in 1970s photographs taken in Abiquiu, New Mexico, by her new assistant, Juan Hamilton.

Stieglitz's photographs and ideas were the beginning of many changes in O'Keeffe's life. Now that she was working full time as an artist, her life became inextricably bound to her ability to create; more than ever, she limited her friendships and relationships to those that satisfied her. Stieglitz, on the other hand, was stimulated by discussions and extended correspondence, and O'Keeffe was often present, at first, during his mealtime and evening conversations with artists, writers, and philosophers.

Stieglitz and his friends talked too much to suit O'Keeffe. Nevertheless, these discussions helped to pave the way for new movements in photography and art, including her own acceptance as an artist. Two writers who were inspired by these visual trends were William Carlos Williams and Gertrude Stein, who pioneered the use of American, rather than British, idioms and images. Williams's motto, "No ideas but in things," and Stein's saying, "Rose is a rose is a rose is a rose," exemplified the new use of concrete images to convey ideas. Williams's essays on American history and the American spirit *In the American Grain* and Hart Crane's American epic poem "The Bridge" were both dedicated to Stieglitz. These writers brought the mirror of art so close to nature that each image enlarged, opened up, and revealed something new.

Artists and writers were exchanging ideas and influencing each other's works more than at any other period in American history, and O'Keeffe was no longer on the sidelines. Williams, a doctor to the working-class populations of Passaic and Paterson, New Jersey, became a leader among diverse writers who later called him the father of modern American poetry. Stein, in Paris, was at the hub of gatherings of artists, including Picasso and Hemingway.[11] And Stieglitz was hosting Sherwood Anderson, Paul Rosenfeld, Waldo Frank, Herbert Seligmann, Williams, Crane, and many other writers at Lake George and in New York. O'Keeffe was literally surrounded by the new thinkers of her generation who were changing the direction of the arts. The period in New York from 1919 to 1929 was her most prolific, as well as being visually rich and varied.

Williams praised Stieglitz's focus on "the immediate and the actual" in America in an essay, "The American Background":

Using his own art, photography, he still, by writing, by patronage, by propaganda and unstinted friendship, carried the fullest load forward. The photographic camera and what it could do were peculiarly well suited to a place where the immediate and the actual were under official neglect.[12]

During the early twenties, Stieglitz's stunning, closeup portraits of O'Keeffe were a great departure from the romantic, soft-focus, manipulated images that had been popular in photography at the turn of the century.

In this vein, Williams, Stieglitz, and many of their classically educated contemporaries discarded and discouraged any nostalgia for past intellectual movements. In a symbolic gesture, Stieglitz gave his collection of 418 early photographs to the Metropolitan Museum in 1933. Even if the romantic tradition did provide visual and moral alternatives to industrialism, no artist wanted to imitate the past. The works of nineteenth-century transcendentalist painters and writers, such as Albert Bierstadt and Ralph Waldo Emerson, received their share of attacks for falling into the trap of leaning on past styles that they were inveighing against. Williams expressed his differences with the romantics in his view of Emerson's failings:

> . . . *one does not disguise one's poverty by enhancing one's appearance through the use of another's spiritual favors.*
>
> *Even an Emerson did not entirely escape, his genius as a poet remaining too often circumscribed by a slightly hackneyed gentility. He did not relate himself so well to the underlying necessity as his style shows him to have been related to the style of the essayists of the older culture—running counter to a world exploding around him. Only at moments did his vigor break through . . .*
>
> *He was a poet, in the making, lost. His spiritual assertions were intended to be basic, but they had not—and they have not today—the authenticity of Emily Dickinson's unrhymes. And she was of the same school, rebelliously.*[13]

An urgency to express compelling and immediate concerns, to invent new spiritual and moral standards, rather than to borrow from the past, permeated the heated discussions carried on by Stieglitz, Williams, and their close associates. As Williams put it:

> *The revolution*
> *is accomplished.*
> *Noble has been*
> *changed to no bull.*[14]

Where should she start? After her experiments with abstract drawings and watercolors, O'Keeffe produced the first oil paintings since her student efforts. Initially in 1918, her manner was modified and controlled, and her compositions of single flowers began as original contributions to the still-life tradition she had studied since childhood. Soon her choice of objects to paint expanded to include two pears, a bowl of apples, and unusual objects with classic forms—an avocado, two figs, a turkey feather, and two ram's horns. Despite her disclaimers, at least some of these objects appear to act as self-evident sexual meta-

phors humorously "one-upping" the symbolic photographic close-ups of Stieglitz, Sheeler, and Strand. In her own way, O'Keeffe continually derived inspiration and subjects from her immediate surroundings throughout her career. Two examples from 1923 show the refined techniques and immediacy of style leading to her 1924 flower portraits. *Dark Leaves* (c. 1923, see

Canna, *1919, oil on cardboard, 11¼" x 8⅛"*

p. 160), is an unusual portrayal of fall foliage; the blue and silver-blue leaves on yellow ground imply that at twilight some leaves have soaked up the sky's blues and reds, leaving the central oak leaf to reflect the last muted silver and gold rays of light. The smooth and serrated leaves become a complex landscape that resembles larger land forms. In *Lake George* (1923, see p. 45), the water, land, and sky shapes are simplified to emphasize their meeting points and similarities. The colors have been reduced to blues and brown with white and ochre highlights. The land form, like the oak leaf in the previous painting, seems to become a focal point conveying a specific mood in this case, a placid serenity. Only the sky seems protean and alive.

The flowers she created epitomize O'Keeffe's growth, magnetism, and energy at this stage in her career. Her choice was influenced by her early training, her attraction to flowers, and the idea of a fresh and fragile thing in the concrete maze of the city.

One favorite early subject was the red canna, a hardy tropical plant with broad leaves. In *Canna* (1919, see p. 55), the red-purple flower with a dark green stem and leaf is centered on a blue ground. The lighter ground spotlights the flower and accents its loneliness and darkness. The flower center, also highlighted, is nevertheless vague, and the center recedes quite naturally from the viewer's eye. This was the first oil painting by O'Keeffe that Stieglitz sold, appropriately, to friends who admired the vibrance and simple harmony of a single flower.

Close observations of O'Keeffe's paintings of flower forms affirm that she never pursued the realist approach. She did not paint every petal and detail, certainly not the usual shadows, in the Dutch still-life tradition; instead, she gave her flowers a life of their own, an expression that changed significantly between 1918 and 1938. O'Keeffe's subsequent red canna paintings gradually enlarged the central flower image and brought it closer to the edges of the canvas, culminating in *Red Canna* (1923, see p. 53), a poetic, charged abstraction dominated by dancing petal forms. O'Keeffe always insisted that she was painting the flower itself, but this does not explain the changes in flower and other images as her ideas and talents matured.

O'Keeffe's paintings of 1919 also returned to the abstract mode that had initially attracted Stieglitz's attention. One deeply impressionistic painting, *Music—Pink and Blue* (1919), shows O'Keeffe at her best. The abstraction is suggestive of her later Pelvis Series in its use of forms but more imaginative in coloration and design.

The composition has three main areas of form—a central arching shape that curves inward; a darker ovoid space in the lower right center; and, above that, the same ovoid inverted above the arch.

White sizing under the smooth surface makes the colors luminous. The two ovoid shapes in different tones of turquoise evoke sea, sky, and other eternal images. The central form is more complex in coloration. The left, wider side of the archway uses blues and pinks alternately, with white edges echoing the curving arch and forming complementary diagonals to it. On the inner edge of the arch, pink hues meld to rose with gray edges. The rose ridges provide a vivid complement to the nearby turquoise oval. The form has a tubular, visceral quality. The warm colors and sensuous lines are controlled yet fluid, earthy yet cerebral. As the title indicates, an inner and outer harmony is evoked. Some joy, some insight is being universalized and celebrated.

As a personal joke, Stieglitz took the curving, erect plaster maquette O'Keeffe made during the early days of their correspondence and photographed it in front of *Music—Pink and Blue*. The unmistakable union of the lingam and yoni—the male and female—emerges. This symbolism was never discussed by either artist but is another indication that their relationship had a very conscious sexual dimension.

Music—Pink and Blue is the crescendo of a melody—O'Keeffe's own tune. This painting, a personal favorite of the artist, remained in her collection for the next fifty years.[15] The painting is perfectly realized; its beauty and deep, suggestive rhythms seem perpetually fresh and young.

In 1919, Oaklawn became too much of a financial burden for Hedwig Stieglitz, who was seventy-five; her husband had died in 1909. Oaklawn was sold that fall. The next summer, the family moved up the hill to the farmhouse that had been the private domain of O'Keeffe and Stieglitz the year before, necessitating closer quarters for themselves and guests. In the city, they moved into his brother Leopold's house at 60 East 65th Street and remained there for four years, running their own household in upstairs quarters. O'Keeffe and Stieglitz were genuinely grateful for Lee's and Lizzie's generosity, which eased their modest financial situation. In the legal arena, Emmy refused Stieglitz's continued requests for a divorce.

During her first summers at Lake George, O'Keeffe became an avid gardener, and she wanted to become a mother. Stieglitz evaded the topic; then a tragedy ended the discussion in 1923. Stieglitz's only daughter suffered postpartum dementia praecox after childbirth. This Smith College graduate, falling often into using the language of a seven-year-old, was institutionalized for the rest of her life. Stieglitz rarely spoke about his daughter Kitty again and was never permitted to visit her, but he sent cards and presents on her birthday and holidays. The issue of having a child with O'Keeffe was permanently closed.[16]

Another problem appeared. Beginning in 1924, illnesses began to stalk both Stieglitz and O'Keeffe; each was ill intermittently until 1935; then O'Keeffe's health improved while Stieglitz continued to battle angina and heart attacks until his death in 1946. O'Keeffe's problems were vague in 1924 and lasted one to two weeks: the "curse," a vaccination causing her feet to swell, a cold, or just "illness" were the ailments Stieglitz mentioned in his letters to friends that year. He also narrated his current setbacks: a fall, a kidney stone, angina, colic, and sinusitis.

Emmy finally granted her estranged husband a divorce at the end of 1924. Stieglitz, sixty, and O'Keeffe, thirty-seven, moved into their own studio at 35 East 58th Street in November and were married on December 11.

Calla Lily, *1927, oil on canvas, 20" x 9"*

In 1925, after six months in the studio, O'Keeffe persuaded Stieglitz to move into a suite on the thirtieth floor of the newly constructed Shelton Hotel on Lexington Avenue near 49th Street. The fine view of the nearby skyscrapers and the East River and the good light for painting provided an impetus to produce new works, notably the first paintings of Manhattan and exotic, enlarged flowers, such as the black iris.

From 1923 through 1928, O'Keeffe's recognition as an artist entered a new stage. Beginning with her exhibitions at the Anderson Galleries in 1923 and 1924—with Stieglitz showing his photographs simultaneously in 1924—O'Keeffe began to receive reviews from Stieglitz's many associates, including Henry McBride, Paul Rosenfeld, and Elizabeth McCausland of *The Springfield Republican*. Later, Edmund Wilson and Lewis Mumford reviewed her exhibitions for the *New York Times* and *The New Yorker*. O'Keeffe often disagreed with the reviews, but Stieglitz, diplomatically mediating between the artist and the critics, continued to encourage the critics.

Lowe has pointed out that Stieglitz's ability "to cajole critics and purchasers derived from having been an active champion of other modernists since 1907," adding, "O'Keeffe's exhibitions were arranged, orchestrated, ballyhooed and celebrated by Stieglitz. Without his efforts, recognition could not possibly have come to her as early as it did."[17] Stieglitz had strong personal principles about selling art only to those whose appreciation was genuine, but he also raised the prices of O'Keeffe's paintings 100 percent between 1918 and 1937, and he cautioned her against low fees for certain commissions and competitions. Her first charcoal had sold for under one hundred dollars in 1918, and was paid for in monthly installments. By 1924, the prices for oil paintings were nearing one thousand dollars, with three thousand five hundred dollars not unreasonable by 1927. He insisted that each painting should have a good home; he did not sell coldly or automatically. The records of sales transactions in his letters reveal that Stieglitz was also willing to bargain—to give discounts to museums or to purchasers of more than one work.

The secrecy and ambiguity that prevailed throughout O'Keeffe's career may be seen in the rumors surrounding the large flower painting installed at the exclusive Elizabeth Arden salon in New York in 1937. The official story was that Arden had commissioned

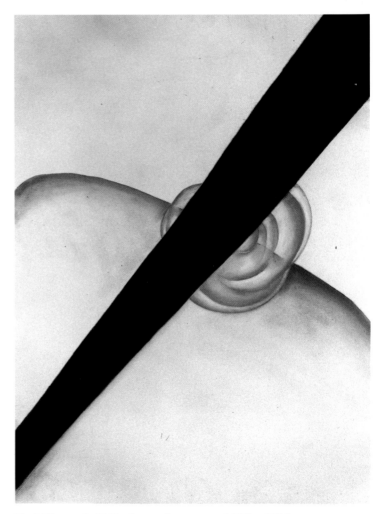

Black Diagonal, *1919, charcoal on paper, 24½" x 19¾"*

the largest oil by O'Keeffe to date, 72 by 84 inches, for ten thousand dollars. This story, in itself, raised O'Keeffe's commercial value. However, Arden's niece recalled that the painting was a gift—that the prominent display in a luxurious setting would serve O'Keeffe's interests. The records are so vague that even the given title of this work, *Jimson Weed,* and the date, 1934, seem imprecise. The painting features one flower similar to the flower in the *White Trumpet Flower* (1932), and three gigantic jimson weeds in three stages of opening (see pp. 48–49). The astonishing brilliance of the four white blossoms is emphasized by the large,

Calla Lilies *by Charles Demuth, 1927, oil on canvas, 14" x 10"*

East River No. 1, *1926, oil on canvas, 12⅛″ x 32⅛″*

soft folds of the azure and green petals and filmy cloud background. Since Arden also purchased two smaller flower paintings for her apartment, it is likely that one or more works was provided at a discount or as a bonus. In the 1980s, the same large painting would be conservatively valued at more than seven hundred thousand dollars. "O'Keeffe knew her value and maintained her value," one of her contemporaries observed.

O'Keeffe's flowers proliferated in all shapes and hues. The 7-by-9-inch masterpiece *Red Poppy* (1927), with intense, China-red petals flowing past the edges of canvas toward the viewer, exemplified the power and scale of even the smallest paintings. The Black Petunia and White Morning Glory Series of 1926, with two contrasting colors competing for attention in the slim vertical format, exhibited the grace and the asymmetrical yet classic shapes of a Chinese brush painting. In the 30-by-36-inch oil *Black Iris*, O'Keeffe reached the zenith in her quest for a perfect flower perfectly realized.

In contrast to the bright, hardy canna portraits, *Black Iris* (1926) is notable for its fragile, evanescent beauty. The polarity of the light upper petals and dark lower petals, the curving diagonals which meet in a central diamond, and the translucent intensity of the flower add to its dynamic unity. The subtle gradations of tone create the delicacy of real petals even though the opaque medium of oil paint has been applied with an intensity and thoroughness seen only in the best paintings by O'Keeffe. The flower seems illuminated from within.

The highlight of the composition is the upward-arching upper portion of the flower with its cathedrallike grandeur. The viewer follows the painter's eye to enter the center of the flower. A tightly curving inner petal in mauve and maroon hues shields the tiny reproductive organs inside as the wide, dark purple lower petal droops downward. Fluid diagonal lines form a central diamond.

The textures in *Black Iris* are not noticeable from a few feet away but do affect the perceived depth of the image. Light crosshatching and extra, tiny diagonal brushstrokes help to create the translucent effect. O'Keeffe used this technique in a few other flower paintings and more rarely in paintings of other subjects. O'Keeffe's art commonly featured smooth-appearing surfaces, a technique that placed optimal emphasis on color and form.

O'Keeffe usually worked directly from nature, but some paintings were also her interpretations of subjects that others in the Stieglitz circle had painted. Charles Demuth's watercolor study *Iris* for the related 1927 oil *Calla Lilies* illustrates this. In Demuth's painting, five stems arch out from a soft spiral of folds protecting the bulb and curve diagonally into each other. A wavy leaf on the far right points toward the central bud and two flowers as a second leaf, flat and horizontal, interrupts the flow of the stems and underscores the flower detail. In the upper right of the composition, two flowerheads curve together, to contrast and balance the base of the plant in the lower left corner. The petals are wrapped around the upward-curving, just-protruding tongues or spadix. The small tongues command attention since the diagonal dynamic of the composition flows toward them. The painting's unity and wry humor are characteristic of Demuth.

O'Keeffe's *Two Calla Lilies on Pink* (1928) is an oil on canvas almost as large as the Demuth lilies—40 by 30 inches as compared to the 42⅛ by 48 inches—but the entire surface is covered by two white flowers whose edges flow off the canvas. The two blossoms are slightly more open than Demuth's, and the bright yellow tongues are more pronounced and less narrow. The resemblance between the two paintings lies in the similarity between the two flowers in each and their diagonal placement. O'Keeffe's portrait has more warmth but less humor. The flowers seem to float on a mauve and pink ground with folds that interrelate with the folds of the petals. The tops of the green stems in the lower right point toward the complementary yellow tongues or spadix.

The edges of the two flowerheads form the main diagonals of the composition, with pink ground in the four corners and middle. The flower bodies or spathes are shaded in light tones of

Shell and Shingle VI, *1926, oil on canvas, 30¹/₁₆″ x 17⁷/₈″*

yellow and green, with the folds lightly edged in blue-green and gray. The flowers have a placid surface, cool and impenetrable. The lightly crosshatched surface is solid and hard, in direct contrast to the effect in *Black Iris*. From the receding center of each flower, a bold orange-yellow spadix emerges. As they jut out at different angles toward the top and left centers, the erect tongues dominate the composition.

This lack of subtlety was one of the reasons O'Keeffe's art appealed to the public, but not to all critics. One side effect of the blatant imagery was its unpredictable effect on different viewers. One woman removed a flower painting by O'Keeffe from her living room when she found her husband using it to illustrate a sex education lesson to her child. After she relocated the painting in the bedroom, a friend remarked, "Oh, I'm so glad you took that vagina off the wall." One critic went even further, interpreting the pistil protruding from the flowers as the clitoris. Although this view ignored the fact that the two parts are not functionally analogous, O'Keeffe's increased sensitivity in the 1920s to the sexual centers of flower paintings is undeniable![18] O'Keeffe's flowers, leaves, and fees were emphasized in a friendly portrait by Demuth, who painted still-life caricatures of all of the artists in the Stieglitz circle.

O'Keeffe's paintings of New York City and Lake George were just as eye-opening as her flowers. The city paintings made between 1925 and 1929 rely heavily on geometric design. Usually a dominant vertical or horizontal shape is depicted in black and white tones; sparks of color symbolize night life.

Shelton Hotel, New York, No. 1 (1926, see p. 72) is the most realistically depicted skyscraper. All twenty-four floors, in potato-skin brown and mustard-brown tones, abut a gray-and-white sky; neighboring towers zoom in to add dark triangles to the upper edges of the composition. The three doors in oval archways at the entrance and three big windows of the apartment where Stieglitz and O'Keeffe lived are emphasized at the lower and upper center. The white-toned window rectangles spaced across the building

have an unusual dimension, as noted by O'Keeffe connoisseur Myron Kunin: "The clever part of it is that she is showing reflections in those windows that are all different—there are quite a variety of tones, perhaps reflections of the sky."[19]

O'Keeffe's city paintings, unlike the flowers, were in answer to

Poster Portrait: Georgia O'Keeffe *by Charles Demuth, c. 1925, oil on board, 22⅞" x 16⁷⁄₁₆"*

Sunflower #2, 1935, oil on canvas, 19" x 13"

Lake George Window, *1929, oil on canvas, 40" x 30"*

unspoken challenges from the male artists, especially Charles Sheeler and John Marin, whose interpretations of architectural forms were well known. Stieglitz had exhibited O'Keeffe's Lake George barn, *The Shanty* (1922), in 1923 at the Anderson Galleries, and this was sold to longstanding friend and patron Duncan Phillips for his collection in Washington, D.C. However, the skyscrapers were not included in O'Keeffe's annual exhibitions of 1926 and 1927.

In 1927, O'Keeffe painted *Radiator Building—Night, New York,* a dazzling frontal view of the new, brightly lit building. The black tower glows with dazzling light gray square windows; blue to green city lights stream over the top. This painting captures the gay spirit of the twenties—the power inside and outside the neon-studded tower. She included the only billboard sign she ever painted, replacing the words *Scientific American* with *Alfred Stieglitz.* The red-on-red sign putting Stieglitz on top of the city was a humorous tribute. In 1928, Stieglitz relented and exhibited the New York buildings for the first time.

These continue to receive mixed reviews; former Art Institute of Chicago Director Daniel Catton Rich wrote that O'Keeffe's New York paintings "lack the final quality of transformation" of other works.[20] What *was* missing was the opportunity for greater color and greater linear freedom. O'Keeffe was confined in New York, yet, whether she realized it or not, she was also at her apex as an artist. The works of the late twenties, including the buildings, are among her most satisfying, painterly, and memorable works.

O'Keeffe soon realized that her association with Stieglitz would require her to do much more than paint. The time spent posing before Stieglitz's camera had decreased, due to a lessening in the intensity and quantity of portraits of O'Keeffe. In the twenties, however, she assumed some gallery duties such as framing and hanging shows, and packing and unpacking paintings. To a few friends, she complained about the chores at Stieglitz's Intimate Gallery and, later, at An American Place. Why should she hang Marin's big exhibition at the new Museum of Modern Art as well when he didn't have the courtesy to pick up her handkerchief? More and more, she began to concentrate on framing her own paintings and hanging her own shows.

Stieglitz himself had many personal needs and idiosyncrasies that interfered with her freedom and privacy. He was a finicky dresser and sometimes sent her on shopping errands. As a hospitable entertainer, he often invited friends to dinner in the hotel dining room at Child's, or a favorite Chinese restaurant, and occasionally to linger after dinner to talk. Twenty-three years older and prone to physical ailments, Stieglitz consulted his doctors as often as necessary and sometimes needed special care.

Despite minor illnesses and ups and downs with her husband and his relatives, O'Keeffe produced many memorable works at Lake George. Nevertheless, the emotional climate of the late twenties was not serene for O'Keeffe and Stieglitz, and by the summer of 1928—as described by Lowe—"the strain between them seemed more palpable" than the year before.[21] Finally, O'Keeffe took a month to visit her aunts, who had moved back to Wisconsin. When she returned, her antagonism toward Stieglitz had evaporated.

Among her many abstract and concrete studies of the Lake George landscape are the Shell and Old Shingle Series of 1926 and the Jack-in-the-Pulpit Series of 1930. Each series progresses from realism to abstraction, from the whole to a closer look at one or another of the parts. The shell is reduced to a white teardrop shape on black ground in *Shell and Shingle VI* (see p. 63). This simple composition is comparable to the works that critics began to call "Minimalist" in 1958, indicating that O'Keeffe was not only ahead of her time but also several jumps ahead of the label-prone critics. As always in her work, she portrayed the life within each shape, not the current popular theory.

Reviews of her art were—and remain—the center of a controversy about the role and language of art critics. Did Stieglitz initiate the dilemma by continuing to admire O'Keeffe's art as "a woman on paper"? O'Keeffe's friends Paul Rosenfeld and Lewis Mumford as well as critics Samuel Kootz and Edmund Wilson all made a point of mentioning that O'Keeffe's art was feminine and, therefore, not in the same category as the work of male artists. Edmund Wilson fell into this trap while reviewing a group exhibition at the Anderson Galleries for *The New Republic* on March 18, 1925:

In Miss Georgia O'Keeffe America seems definitely to have produced a woman painter comparable to her best woman poets and novelists . . .

Georgia O'Keeffe outblazes the other painters in the exhibition—Marin, Hartley, Dove and Demuth—but it is impossible to compare her with them—even in those pictures which are closest to hers: the white-silver and black storm-clouds of Dove. If the art of women and the art of men have, as I have suggested, fundamental differences, they sometimes seem incommensurable. The water-colors of Mr. Marin are masculine masterpieces: they are the investiture of nature with the distinction of a distinguished temperament: some of the Maine seascapes, with their greens and blues and white sails, with their incomparable combination of dryness with freshness, are among the finest Marins I have seen . . .

Lewis Mumford elaborated his view that O'Keeffe "beautified the sense of what it is to be a woman" one year later in his review "O'Keeffe and Matisse" in *The New Republic.*[22] He evaded a direct discussion of the formal qualities of O'Keeffe's art. His metaphor spoke in terms of sensed womanhood rather than art; he implied that womanhood had not been expressed in previous art. This viewpoint excluded other women artists, including Mary Cassatt, and ignored the fact that O'Keeffe had already painted "masculine" subjects—skyscrapers, shingles, barns, canyons, and still lifes.

O'Keeffe's brilliant, centered, deliciously fragile flower detail sparked sexual fantasies in many viewers. In the progressive, daring era of the twenties, an unnamed mystery already surrounded

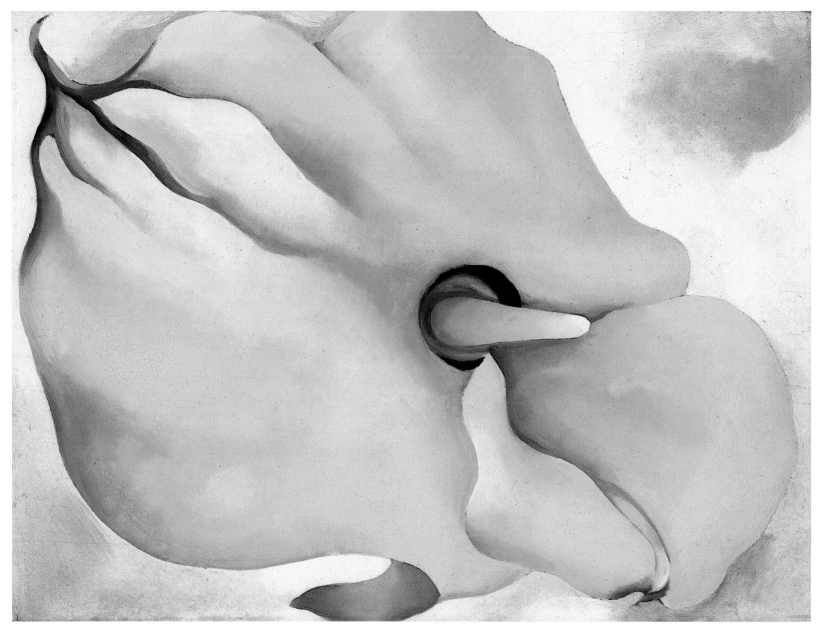

Yellow Calla, *1926, oil on fiberboard, 11¾" x 12¾"*

Pink Sweet Peas, *1927, pastel, 27¹/₃" x 21³/₄"*

O'Keeffe and her paintings, and the paintings of flowers epito-mized the public's view of the artist. As two anonymous reviewers told readers of *Art News:*

Seeking for a cause for this apparent paradox—extreme color selectivity wedded to an almost entire absence of design, we are forced to a conclusion that runs full counter to the generally ac-cepted view. All the critical literature which has been devoted to O'Keeffe—and there has been plenty—has started with the as-sumption that the work of O'Keeffe is first, last and all the time autobiographical . . . Self-revelatory as she may be, she is also—and in the highest degree—a naturalist. Her most seeming ab-stract pictures are only by elimination abstract. They are not only based on nature, they copy nature, line almost for line . . . Willingly or unwillingly, she has bound herself down to a copy book with a fidelity that approaches, and this particularly in her most abstract canvases, the photographic. So restricted, the marvel is not that O'Keeffe at times falls short of the full and complete expression of her gifts promised, but that she is able, as time and again she is, to throw off her trammels and sing. What saves her is her habit of painting the same things, flowers, trees, lakes, land-scapes, over and over again, until they cease to be flowers in a vase before her, to become flowers within her. Look, only look, at the series of petunias in the present exhibition, how they grow, in richness, in intensity, in volume. Never sang a single individual petunia with the rich fullness of that final flower. Its song is the song of the race.

We need never fear for the flowers and the leaves. There O'Keeffe is master.

(Art News, *Vol. 24, February 13, 1926*)

. . . her perennial flowering is each year more fresh than the last. One recognizes the flower but it grows in beauty.

(Art News, *Vol. 26, 1928*)

Black Iris (1926) became noted for its sensual suggestiveness, but O'Keeffe insisted that she was representing the flower itself and flatly denied that the flower was a metaphor for female geni-talia. Feminist critic Linda Nochlin argued, with equal insistence, that the flowers were morphological analogs of female sexual organs.[23] It is ironic that Freudian commentaries in the twenties and one feminist theory fifty years later both pointed to sexual symbolism that O'Keeffe adamantly denied throughout her ca-reer. O'Keeffe's rejection of this view also has its psychological side. Sex was a private, not a public, matter.

As her success as an artist increased, O'Keeffe demanded per-sonal privacy. She had already revealed so much to Stieglitz's cam-era—and the world—that to talk about her life and art seemed redundant. O'Keeffe was not prone to sharing her subconscious or conscious motives with others. If the men discussed Freud's theories about dreams and unconscious influences, that was their business.

Meyer Schapiro's discussion of this issue in Cézanne's art seems applicable to O'Keeffe's flowers:

To rest with the explanation of the still-life as a displaced sexual interest is to miss the significance of still-life in general as well as important meanings of the objects on the manifest plane.[24]

The fact that O'Keeffe's art was discussed in terms of masculine and feminine polarities should be examined in the context of the twenties. The art world in general and Stieglitz's circle in par-ticular were male-dominated. Most professional artists were men; virtually all museum directors, curators, critics, and gallery owners were men. Women often bought art, influenced sales, or worked in supportive roles. There were no women role models as O'Keeffe was developing. She chose to believe that her ideas were new rather than to admit that she had been influenced by any of the hundreds of great artists she met throughout her lifetime.

Other American women artists of O'Keeffe's generation were

still unknown. Portraitist Alice Neel was an art student in Philadelphia; sculptor Louise Nevelson was studying voice, piano, painting, and Eastern metaphysics in New York. The now-reclusive New Mexico–based abstract expressionist painter Agnes Martin was a child in Canada. These women artists gained wide recognition decades later, after working independently for half a century. O'Keeffe's recognition as an artist came sooner, when she was in her early thirties.

O'Keeffe was the only major woman artist of her generation both to pose nude and to allow the resulting photographs to be exhibited. Later in the century, American women artists who either used their own bodies as part of their art or whose art contained explicit sexuality, did so deliberately. Artists such as Louise Bourgeois, Lynda Benglis, and Judy Chicago have stated that they were exploring the myths surrounding sexuality. In Chicago's case, the focus on female, rather than male, attitudes toward sexuality, birth, and women's sensibilities was directly influenced by her study of O'Keeffe's works. In comparison to writers Virginia Woolf and Anaïs Nin, Chicago wrote, "O'Keeffe is the only one of the three who resisted articulating her commitment to a female art, despite the fact that her work clearly reflects that commitment." [25] Chicago's definition of female art is not fixed; she indicates that it begins with each artist: "Their self-images did not correspond to society's definition of women. Asserting their own self-definitions was an implicit step toward challenging the culture and demanding that it adjust its definition of women to correspond to women's lives, a demand that was not even apprehended, much less met." [26] O'Keeffe's images seem to be self-definitions in the broad sense that they have gender associations based upon their nature, colors, and form.

Close readings of the ongoing changes in O'Keeffe's flower paintings as prototypes lend credence to arguments favoring literal and figurative interpretations. Impressionistic dashes of cobalt blue centered on a white ground in 1917, magnified flower centers in the 1920s, and emblems of the desert terrain in the 1930s each contain natural vitality, vigor, and beauty. Yet a flower, like a cloud, is evanescent. O'Keeffe's art is never one-dimensional. Chicago's term *self-definition* suggests subconscious and intuitive, as well as literal, biographical correspondences.

O'Keeffe was primarily creating self-definitions of the object itself. Each flower, leaf, and skyscraper had its own character and vitality, true to the Williams motto "No ideas but in things." She limited the concerns she addressed and chose her subjects carefully, developing her own emblems/icons/archetypes—her equivalents. Sometimes O'Keeffe and Stieglitz competed for images; when he was the first to photograph the door at the farmhouse, she was the first to paint the window. However, when Stieglitz photographed clouds and when O'Keeffe painted clouds, there was no simple formula, no single definition or meaning. Every work contained its own individuality and message.

The focus in the flower paintings shifted in the 1930s and 1940s. More moods and attitudes were evident in flowers that were either large and hearty or tiny and artificial. The Sunflower Series, done in 1936, had the thickly painted richness of a Van Gogh sunflower with its lucid yellow petals plastered against the bright-toned blue sky of the Southwest. The visible brushstrokes have a strong, diagonal vigor and lead the eye from the upward-curving green leaves to the windblown petals and the yellow, brown, and green spotted circle of seeds that form a central eye. The flower seems brighter, more alive than an ordinary sunflower.

The same can be said for *Daffodils* (1937), also done in bright yellows, with orange and greens. Two paintings of the night-blooming, poisonous desert plant, *Jimson Weed* (1934) and *Two Jimson Weeds* (1938), are such enlarged versions of reality that they become bold, mysterious fantasies. In *Jimson Weed,* the petals, as expansive as white clouds, and the dark aqua center and seeds contain the essence of exotic but deadly beauty. *Narcissa's Last Orchid,* a pastel done in 1941, is another frontal plunge into the flower's center. The realism of the serrated petal edges heightens the impact of the extruding central pod. These flower centers

New York Night, *1928–1929, oil on canvas, 40" x 19"*

Shelton Hotel, New York, No. 1, *1926, oil on canvas, 32" x 17"*

East River from the Thirtieth Story of the Shelton Hotel, New York, *1928, oil on canvas, 30″ x 48″*

Poppy, *1927, oil on canvas, 30" x 36"*

Poppies, *1950, oil on canvas, 36″ x 30″*

Georgia O'Keeffe and Orville Cox, Canyon de Chelly National Monument, *Arizona, 1937, photograph by Ansel Adams*

4. Ghost Ranch: O'Keeffe and Adams

The summer of 1929 was another turning point in O'Keeffe's life. As a guest of effervescent socialite and arts patron Mabel Dodge Luhan in Taos, New Mexico, O'Keeffe, accompanied by Rebecca Strand, stayed in a small adobe house set off by itself near a large piñon pine towering over the landscape. Mabel had lured her favorite writer, D. H. Lawrence, his wife, Frieda, and their deaf friend, artist Lady Brett Esher, from England to Kiowa Ranch in 1924. Lawrence got a Mexican carpenter and three Indians to help repair the house and build three small cabins. Lawrence and Frieda moved on to Italy in 1925. A metal phoenix emblem tacked onto the broad pine trunk reminds visitors of that bird's mythic connection with the sky, not to mention Lawrence's flight from Mabel's roost. Mabel's salon gatherings in Paris and New York were attended by leading artists, writers, and musicians, many of whom were also friends of Stieglitz and O'Keeffe. John Marin, Gertrude Stein, Ansel Adams, and Picasso were among her diverse acquaintances. Mabel moved from New York to Taos in 1917, the same year that Stieglitz closed 291. As an arts patron, Mabel was a pivotal personage. She had attracted many people who should be together, and she continued to invite artists to be her guests in Taos.

Now that she was married to Navajo Tony Luhan, her ranch was a western retreat for her many friends. Tony was a quiet, thoughtful man whose Indian heritage gave him a strong love of the land. O'Keeffe shared his appreciation of nature and got along better with Tony than with Mabel. She and Rebecca went camping with him more than once.

O'Keeffe and Mabel were opposites in almost every way. Mabel was flirtatious, gossipy, pushy, and sophisticated. O'Keeffe, never one to meddle in the affairs of others, abhorred the jealous scenes played out by the three women she knew in New Mexico—for Mabel, Dorothy Brett, and Frieda all loved Lawrence. The competition for his affection and attention was fierce. Mabel was so eager to keep Lawrence nearby that she had deeded Kiowa Ranch, worth one thousand dollars, to Frieda. Lawrence's friends were

Black Place No. 1, *1944, oil on canvas, 26″ x 30⅛″*

From the White Place, *1940, oil on canvas, 30″ x 24″*

shocked to learn that, in return, he had given Mabel the original manuscript of *Sons and Lovers.* Even his death did not lessen Mabel's determination to have a piece of her favorite writer. She was so eager to have his ashes that his wife resorted to mixing them into a cement block placed in a shrine built for him at the ranch. Frieda couldn't prevent the impassioned memoir on Lawrence that Mabel insisted on writing and publishing. When she turned her sharp pen and tongue in O'Keeffe's direction, Mabel hypothesized that her artist friend was sexually repressed—what other explanation could there be for art with full-blown, thinly disguised sexual symbolism?[1] Lawrence's paintings of nudes, in comparison, were cool portraits. Worldly Mabel wondered if Stieglitz was satisfying his younger wife or exploiting her. O'Keeffe tried to ignore the impropriety of the whole issue of her sexual nature. The rediscovered spacious vistas and color-filled sights of the Southwest enlivened all of her senses and gave her new ideas for canvases. She steered clear of Mabel.

O'Keeffe was "intoxicated" with the power of learning to drive a car toward the endless horizon, and the beauty of *seeing* the desert vistas. The dry, clean mountain air at eight thousand feet and the bold desert colors were a welcome change from the humid green landscape at Lake George. The land and the night sky reminded her of Canyon, Texas. She painted her view of the stars seen through the spiraling limbs of the great pine in *The Lawrence Tree.* Lawrence aptly described the tree as "a great pillar of pale, flaky–ribbed copper," with the wind "hissing in the needles like a nest of serpents."[2]

The quality of the light, the mild climate, and the primitive natural landscape around Taos made it a haven for landscape artists and others who wanted to experience the "golden mean" of the town. The name Taos came from the Chinese word tao, or golden way, according to Mabel. Since the Tewa Indians were in Taos long before artists became attracted to the site, it is likely that the name originated among the Tewa; possibly the site was named after the word for people, *towa,* also the name for their tribe.[3] The Tewa rituals, symbols, dances, and pottery bore similarities to those of the ancient Yang-shao tribes of northern China, which predated the Taoists by centuries. Yet no anthropologist to date has confirmed direct linkages of these cultures. Mabel was a typical Taos resident, freely alluding to Indian and Oriental influences and sometimes mixing them up.

Paul Rosenfeld, Marsden Hartley, and the Strands were among those who had already visited Mabel. John Marin, who also visited that summer, created rhythmic, light-filled watercolors of the corn dance at Santo Domingo, the colorful Sangre de Cristo foothills and mountains, and various local sites. Hartley had worked in oils on *Mountain with Cemetery* and other somber compositions featuring heavy crosses and mountains in white, reds, browns, and black. Hartley was probably not aware that he used the Tewa cardinal colors: white = above, red = east, and black = below. The sky and land shapes and colors were a microcosm, a summation, nature's palette. Artists who populated Taos included Joseph Imhof, who chose to live on the Taos Reservation to paint and study Indian life; Russian Nicolai Fechin, a portraitist of the French Post-Impressionist school who painted writer Willa Cather's portrait when she visited Taos; Latvian painter Maurice Sterne, who was known for his paintings from Bali and Egypt and who had moved to Taos with Mabel; and the Paris-born, New York-educated artist Andrew Dasburg, who visited Taos often and settled there in 1930. The Taos artists were worldly romantics, able to appreciate the cultures and rituals of the Indian tribes in the vicinity and to keep abreast of the art news from Paris, New York, London, and Asia.

O'Keeffe extended her stay for three months, bought her first Ford for painting and camping expeditions, and began to explore the territory. She was not overly sociable; her first meetings with pianist/photographer Ansel Adams, future museum director Daniel Catton Rich, writer Mary Austin, and Taos socialites like

Mabel did not impress her. More important were camping trips with Tony and Rebecca, and the resurgence of her desire—and need—to paint.

The effect of the New Mexico landscape on O'Keeffe as an artist has been summarized by art historian Beaumont Newhall, who moved from New York to New Mexico himself:

Number one is the light. Two is the expanse, the vastness of the land. Three is the colors of the landscape; light itself intensifies the colors. In photography, light is so strong that the shadows become very dark. It is probably that physical environment factor that dragged—dragged—O'Keeffe to the West. Also, to an Easterner, it's hard to believe that there are parts of the country that have so few people.

I've also developed a different view of distance and think nothing of traveling 110 miles to get someplace. The scenery constantly changes; there is no traffic or lights.[4]

O'Keeffe's paintings of the next ten years were unprecedented in the history of art. Her representations of hills, bones, crosses, and adobe churches were an original infusion into the still-life and Post-Impressionist traditions that O'Keeffe had studied at the Art Institute of Chicago and the New York Art Students League. Although Vincent Van Gogh's painting *Old Church Tower at Nuenen* (1885) had never been exhibited in America or seen by O'Keeffe, this work has elements in common with O'Keeffe's new work. Her Ranchos de Taos Church Series (1929–1930) and Van Gogh's *Tower* both focus on a protruding part of the edifice with the building, ground, and sky completing the composition. Van Gogh's tower is the solitary, dominant image as wild flowers and blackbirds—evanescent symbols of spring and death—hover nearby.

O'Keeffe's Ranchos Church Series highlights the extended nave of the church, with its two L-shaped wings in shadows. Sun-bleached earth and turquoise-blue sky surround the building.

Georgia O'Keeffe in the Garden at Ghost Ranch, *1948, photograph by Philippe Halsman. Copyright Philippe Halsman*

Ranchos Church No. 1, *1929, oil on canvas, 18¾" x 24"*

Ranchos Church Taos, New Mexico, *1930, oil on canvas, 24" x 36"*

Front of Ranchos Church

There are no signs of life; distance, cloud cover, and sunlight are the main variables in the different views of the curving walls of the hand-finished adobe church. O'Keeffe uses the same subtle textured effect found in *Black Iris;* visible diagonal brushstrokes add a compressed dimensionality to church and sky.

Art historian Robert Rosenblum views Van Gogh's series of the church tower at Nuenen as "the kind of passionate search for religious truths in the world of empirical observation that characterizes so many of the Northern Romantics . . ." and as ". . . something about the profound, unchanging relationships of religion to humble toil, to the daily cycles of work and nature."[5] O'Keeffe, as usual, did not state her intention, but the Ranchos Church Series is clearly an expression of faith, of human capability to create out of earth and sky forms that contain beauty and meaning.

While most critics noted a new realism and closeness to nature, her forte was, more than ever, the selection and abstraction of a particular object or view. In the bright New Mexico sunshine, her

Back of Ranchos Church

art attained a new earth-centered quality. O'Keeffe was back in her element, away from her confining, high-pressure city life. *Abstraction* (1929, see p. 92) juxtaposes three dark silhouettes, one with two red-orange patches. Was O'Keeffe literally hiding and showing her wounds from Stieglitz's affair with Norman?

During a visit to a rodeo with Rebecca Strand, Tony Luhan, and his Indian friends, O'Keeffe found the ride along dirt roads in a convertible to be vaguely reminiscent of the Texas desert, but more exciting. The Indians were wearing sheets and covered their heads and faces when passing through towns. At Santa Clara pueblo, they went to get ready for the dance. Tony told the two women to enjoy themselves and he went off to take his place at the drums. When one dancer came toward them, O'Keeffe was fascinated by his circular ornament of feathers and tiny mirrors spinning and flashing in the sunlight. This is the mysterious, rainbow-colored circle dominating her large painting *At the Rodeo* (1929, see p. 93). The image, enlarged and spiraling in the artist's eyes and memory, is not realistically recognizable, yet it conveys the symbolic unity of the dancers and nature—sun, sky, earth—and the spirit of the occasion.

A more common and somber symbolic image was the wooden cross that ardent sects of Spanish Catholics called *penitentes* had erected as they invaded Indian territory in the 1800s. They had forced their religion upon the natives, but now the church's widespread domination of the Southwest was taken for granted. This point of view is implicit in O'Keeffe's painting *Black Cross, New Mexico* (1929). A heavy, black cross with wooden pegs looms in front of the endless desert hills luminous with rose and yellow layers of light at sunset. Among the many meanings proposed, critic Mahonri Sharp Young has interpreted *Black Cross* grimly in his remark, "The dark, violent underside of life appeals to her."[6] As images of crucifixion and death, the cross and skulls were age-old still-life symbols, yet O'Keeffe presented them in a lively, nontraditional manner.

O'Keeffe was acutely aware of the Catholic church's power to dominate the land by controlling its many pious inhabitants. It was no coincidence that O'Keeffe spent ten years negotiating the purchase of an abandoned Catholic mission for her second home in Abiquiu in 1945. It had the best view, an enclosed garden, hand-carved doors, a surrounding wall, and the prime location in the mesa town. O'Keeffe was proud to finally occupy the seat of power once held by the Catholic church even if the rundown building was being used as a pigsty at the time of purchase.

O'Keeffe was also pondering her own and Stieglitz's mortality and at the same time clearly searching for new images to express her growing need to become independent of Stieglitz. Nature was omnipresent and primitive, and the colorful wasteland suited her mood and her artistic needs. She began to paint hills, bones, and trees, beginning a new dialogue with herself and a new stage of her career as an artist. She found a new stillness within herself, regaining her lost sense of humor and her health at the same time that something within her, a deep attachment to Stieglitz, was becoming brittle with the realization that she did not share his attachment to his new gallery and life in New York.

As an abstraction, the cross blocks the unseen beauty of the earth's wasteland, the desert. The central, straight-edged (but hand-hewn) dark cross contrasts with the bright, curving hills in the four "windows" behind it, presenting the confrontation of two different worlds and views. The painting shows the fierce attraction of opposites that poet/artist William Blake called contraries. Blake's poem "The Marriage of Heaven and Hell" and his visionary art probed eternal paradoxes, such as "Opposition is true friendship." Heaven and hell were vaguely represented in the endless hills (nature) and the symbols of the cross (religion). Earth forms always resembled body parts in her archetypal imagination—her own self-portraits. However, O'Keeffe denied symbolic interpretations because the meanings were not one-dimensional. As in Blake, heaven and hell, innocence and experience, came in many forms.

The ideas of two close friends of O'Keeffe's may have contrib-

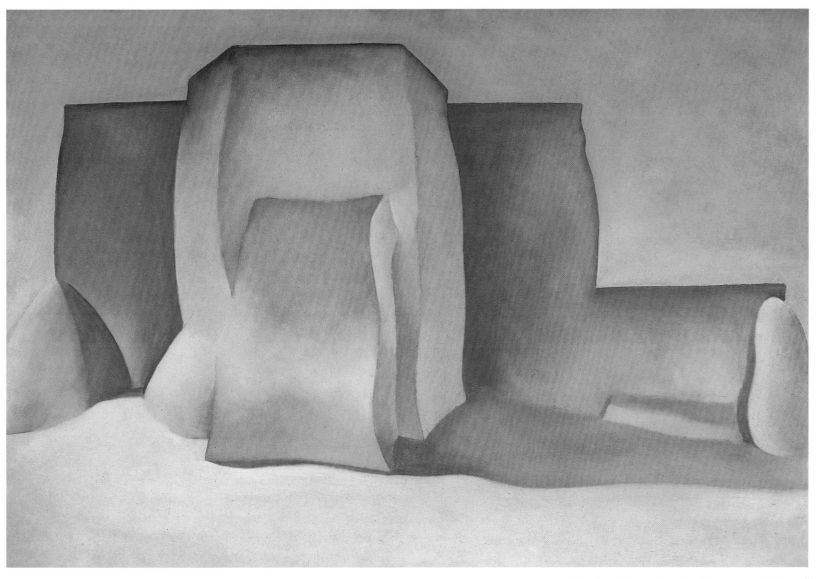

Ranchos Church, *1930, oil on canvas, 24" x 36"*

uted to *Black Cross, New Mexico*. The same head-on view of the same cross is seen in a photograph by her friend Cady Wells. O'Keeffe probably both accompanied Wells to the site near Taos, behind Mabel's Big House on the Penitente Calvary, and kept a copy of his photograph. The undulating, multihued, rounded hill forms first appear in two 1926 oil paintings by Arthur Dove: *Sea Gull Motif* and *Moon and Sea II*. In all likelihood, Stieglitz and O'Keeffe saw and exhibited these Dove works between 1926 and 1929. O'Keeffe always hung the exhibitions of Dove, her favorite among Stieglitz's artist friends.[7]

O'Keeffe's paintings of the New Mexico desert, mesas, and Pedernal Mountain were striking in coloration. Concerning her use of color, art historian Lloyd Goodrich has noted:

It varies so, the way her subject matter is varied. You get those pictures as extraordinary in color as Black Cross, New Mexico, *which is so stark and so startling in its contrast of the sunset to the black cross, and you get other pictures which are much softer— not soft in the derogatory sense, but soft in color. In the pictures of the surface of the earth as seen from the air, the general color quality is different, it seems to me, compared to pictures as dramatic as that black cross, or all the cross pictures.*[8]

Beaumont Newhall has added:

In the South of France, will you see Van Gogh's color? I think that what Van Gogh saw in the South of France and what O'Keeffe saw in the Southwest of America triggered this exaggeration. But this exaggeration is part of what makes art. When someone told Turner he had never seen a sunset as beautiful as the artist's painting, Turner replied, "Don't you wish you had?"[9]

O'Keeffe's color has been discussed in less favorable terms by a few critics, who have noted that most of her early oil paintings, and a few done in the late fifties, did not achieve the rich color balance of her most celebrated works. On the whole, Newhall and Goodrich agree that O'Keeffe's imaginative use of color was a primary achievement. While O'Keeffe's forms have been imitated, her palette has remained simple, fresh, and unique. Correspondingly, the public's attraction to O'Keeffe's use of color has both psychological and aesthetic grounds.

Fascinated by desert vistas after her summer in Taos, O'Keeffe shipped a barrel of bones back East. The desert was keenly alive in her mind as she began to paint the aged, sun-bleached skulls of cattle in detached space, abstract backgrounds, and remembered desert vistas.

Her invigorating experiences in New Mexico did nothing to alleviate her discomfort back in New York due to the evident emotional attachment of Stieglitz and Dorothy Norman. By the time that An American Place opened, due to Norman's organizational and fund-raising efforts, on December 15, 1929, O'Keeffe had become restless and uninspired. The first exhibition was forty-six new watercolors by John Marin. O'Keeffe seemed uninterested in presenting new paintings. Her thirty-five canvases exhibited on February 4, 1930, included, for the first time, works from previous years.

Nevertheless, between 1929 and 1930, O'Keeffe completed the Taos Church Series, the Jack-in-the-Pulpit Series, and many paintings of desert hills and flowers. In 1931, she began a series featuring a cow's skull. Two particular paintings of cow's skulls had opposite feelings and natures that seem to be meditations on polarities, including illusions/realities and male/female identities. Both works feature a cow's skull in the upper center of an abstract background with a vertical black stripe behind the head. In *Cow's Skull: Red, White, and Blue*, bright red stripes down each side of the painting attract each other, leading the viewer's eye from the dark horn tips overlapping the red to the off-white skull. The head is surrounded by a sky-blue downward-pointing triangle whose sides merge with soft, cloud-white upward-pointing triangles.

Cow's Skull: Red, White, and Blue was O'Keeffe's Great American Painting, an emblem for the America she felt she knew better than the male artists of her acquaintance who were always talking

Dark Abstraction, *1924, oil on canvas, 24⅞" x 20⅞"*

about creating the Great American Novel or Painting. Since Stieglitz had helped initiate the movement to recognize and support American artists, other circles of American artists, like the Ashcan School (sometimes called the New York Realists), were gaining wider audiences. Surrealist approaches were being introduced by foreign-born artists who had emigrated to America, such as Armenian painter Arshile Gorky and Mexican satirist Marius De Zayas, a friend and colleague of Stieglitz. Just as visual experimentation was taking American art in different directions, diverse writers, including William Carlos Williams, Sherwood Anderson, Gertrude Stein, and Robert Frost, were using American idioms, language, and settings. The fervent outcry for American art was nationwide. So, O'Keeffe used patriotic colors her own way to create an emblem of the American scene. The red, white, blue, and black painting of a cow's skull is both realistic and visionary, O'Keeffe's brilliant composite of the diversity of styles that followed Post-Impressionist art. Her feminine version, *Cow's Skull with Calico Roses,* was much lighter in tone. On a ground of gray-white, the white skull is adorned with white calico roses at the right horn and nose.

O'Keeffe foresaw that the critics would discuss the life-and-death symbolism of the paintings, and perhaps their haunting surreal aspects. The dreamlike, visionary quality of the detached skulls was O'Keeffe's personal expression of a mood that was widespread in the collapsed economy of the Depression. Since her psychological malaise and minor operation in August of 1927, Stieglitz was always giving his friends updates on O'Keeffe's health; some critics suggested that the suspended skulls were emblems of her mental anguish. No critic or artist discussed her work in terms of the skull's long-standing use in the still-life tradition or commented on O'Keeffe's innovative selection of animal, rather than human, models. The perfect composition and execution of these works show her technical control and underlying strength during a difficult period.

O'Keeffe and Stieglitz were apart for most of the year; as she

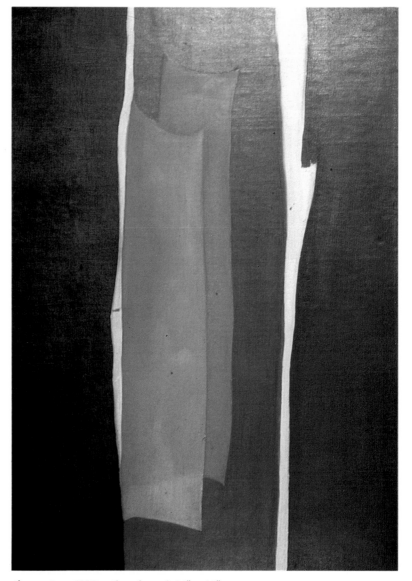

Abstraction, *1929, oil on board, 21" x 15"*

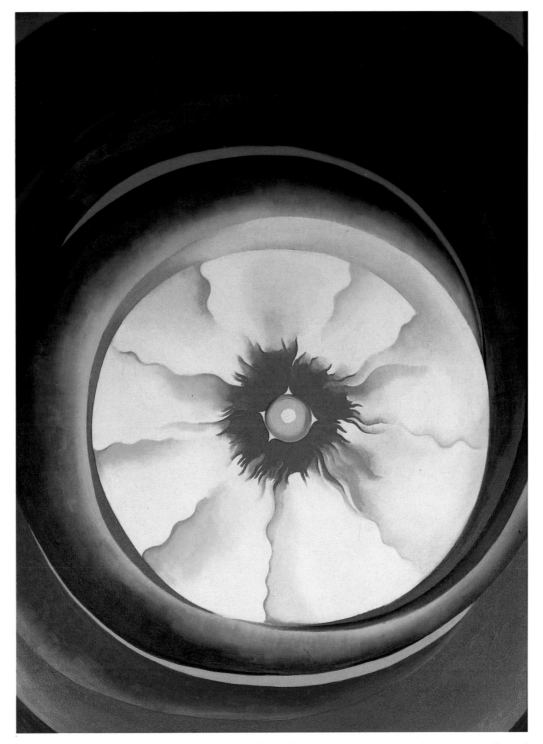

At the Rodeo, New Mexico, *1929, oil on canvas, 40″ x 30″*

painted in New Mexico, Stieglitz was at Lake George with his friends. He even felt well enough to visit Dorothy Norman at her summer house in Woods Hole, Massachusetts. O'Keeffe knew about this visit and the frequent phone conversations between Norman and Stieglitz. She was bitterly jealous. Norman had formally taken over the business duties at An American Place, and Stieglitz had begun to photograph her, correspond, and talk or visit daily. O'Keeffe's needs, and Stieglitz's, were taking them in different directions. A willful artistic spirit is central to O'Keeffe's skull portraits. Any speculations about her fascination with death must revolve around the morbid question, Whose?

Although her paintings indicated new dimensions as an artist, O'Keeffe suffered from depressions in 1931 and 1932. In 1931, she shunned the livelier pace of Taos and rented a cottage on Marie Garland's ranch in Alcalde in April. She spent only one week at the end of July at Lake George, fleeing to York Beach, Maine, for three weeks. On October 11, O'Keeffe returned to Lake George from New York without Stieglitz. In 1932, O'Keeffe, against Stieglitz's advice that the fee was too low, entered and won a competition to paint a mural at Radio City Music Hall, scheduled to open on December 27. Instead of going to New Mexico to paint, she drove with Stieglitz's niece Georgia Engelhard to the Gaspé Peninsula in Canada and painted several large canvases of austere white barns. After two months at Lake George with Stieglitz, she returned to New York City in December to find that the domed ceiling and new plaster in the powder room at the Music Hall would not support her canvas. The cave-in of the mural space, symbolic of the inner turmoil O'Keeffe was experiencing, led her to become hysterical and suffer a nervous breakdown.[10]

O'Keeffe's symptoms—blinding headaches, fits of crying and depression—were diagnosed differently by Stieglitz's brother Lee and the specialists who were called in. She spent five weeks in New York at the house of her sister Anita O'Keeffe Young and her husband, who was the new president of the Pennsylvania Railroad. Anita then put her under the care of a psycho-

neurotherapist, and O'Keeffe was hospitalized for the next two months. In March, O'Keeffe left for Bermuda and did not see Stieglitz again until the end of May. Her friend Marjorie Content, with her teen-age daughter, picked up O'Keeffe at the hospital on the way to the ship. All three were seasick and saw each other again when the ship docked in Bermuda. Marjorie and her daughter explored the islands on bicycles while O'Keeffe recuperated in relative isolation.

Stieglitz felt some guilt for O'Keeffe's illness. She did not begin to recover until the very end of 1933. His acknowledged friendship with Dorothy Norman had begun in 1926 when she was twenty-one, and he now championed her budding talent as a poet and her virtues as a human being just as he had done with O'Keeffe. As he photographed Dorothy in the 1930s, her simple, classic hairstyle and black dress with white at the neckline were superficially reminiscent of the 1917 photographs of O'Keeffe. Another similarity was the situation: Stieglitz's wife Emmy had thrown him out of the house when she caught him photographing O'Keeffe, but now, as O'Keeffe found the same situation—with Norman as subject—Stieglitz told O'Keeffe to leave. Just as she and Stieglitz had not been innocent during the first photography sessions, O'Keeffe probably realized that these new sessions were for art but also were Stieglitz's way of expressing his closeness to and affection for Norman. *Dorothy Norman, 1932* is a Stieglitz portrait that is personal. Norman, with shoulders and chest bare, is seen against a pillow with a sheet modestly concealing her breasts. Her slightly open lips and large, direct eyes seem apprehensive and questioning.[11] O'Keeffe could not stand to be upstaged in Stieglitz's eyes, even if she did not want to pose for him as often as she had. She refused to speak to Norman or even to remain in the same room if a social occasion inadvertently put them together. This was a signal that her days of living with Stieglitz were coming to an end.

Norman's presence was, in many ways, the opposite of O'Keeffe's. Her large, innocent eyes, clear, thoughtful expression, oval face with radiant features, and softer, less angular hands all indicated her own unique personality. Norman also had her own life as a writer, editor, art collector, and wife. Stieglitz admired Norman's literary talents and helped her publish her first book in 1933. She was such an efficient manager of business matters at An American Place that the solicited contributions to the "rent fund" that Stieglitz collected each time he sold a painting were now made out to the Dorothy Norman Rent Fund. Norman, an heiress who never discussed her difficult marriage, was stimulated intellectually and aesthetically by Stieglitz's mentorship. Her two homes in New York City and Woods Hole soon contained works by Stieglitz, Marin, Dove, and Hartley, many selected by Steiglitz as "gifts" in appreciation for her generous efforts in behalf of the Place and its artists. All were tastefully placed in the spacious white-on-white décor, among the seashells and natural objects she collected.

Her association with Stieglitz centered around their mutual high regard for the art of photography. In 1934, Norman helped arrange the publication of *America and Alfred Stieglitz,* a book she had edited with Waldo Frank, Lewis Mumford, Paul Rosenfeld, and Harold Rugg.

The period from 1932 to 1934, when the book was in progress, was a significant turning point in the relationship between O'Keeffe and Stieglitz. He was at another peak in his long and successful career, continuing his voluminous correspondence with colleagues, relatives, artists, patrons, and friends, and, in addition, producing some of his finest photographs of the new skyscrapers in midtown Manhattan. Although he tried to give O'Keeffe the care and attention she needed during the difficult summers of 1932 to 1934, she tired easily and lacked the inspiration to paint. She was bristling and irritable because she needed to be the only woman in Stieglitz's life, and this was no longer the case. Critics rubbed salt into this wound by continuing to probe her works for personal symbolism. By the time Stieglitz realized how painful his attentions to Norman were for O'Keeffe, the dam-

age was irreparable. O'Keeffe's illness served to dampen the intensity of Stieglitz's relationship with Norman. O'Keeffe did not recover easily from this severe blow to her ego. When Stieglitz exhibited photographs of Norman along with those of O'Keeffe in 1932, viewers could not avoid making comparisons, and speculating. His own family publicly acted as though the Norman-Stieglitz friendship was platonic; however O'Keeffe strongly resented Stieglitz's continued esteem for Norman.

In addition, Norman became his first and only protégée behind the camera. Her Graflex prints of Stieglitz at An American Place, skillfully composed and developed, showed a clarity and detail akin to her famous teacher's handiwork. Norman, as Beaumont Newhall has noted, was one of the first American oral historians, recording by hand Stieglitz's personal recollections of significant moments in his life and in photographic history. He left out a few technical points that he no longer considered important; however, his memory was still acute. Norman supplemented his remarks with news clippings, letters, and other documents that she began to collect, finally completing *Alfred Stieglitz: Introduction to an American Seer* in 1960.

Around this time, O'Keeffe herself began to commemorate her husband's photographic achievements. She authorized a small exhibition of Stieglitz's prints at the National Gallery of Art in 1958, a portfolio of Stieglitz's photographs of herself at the Metropolitan Museum in 1978, and in 1983, *Alfred Stieglitz: Photographs and Writings,* coauthored by art historian Sarah Greenough and O'Keeffe's assistant Juan Hamilton. This catalogue and the accompanying exhibition at the National Gallery were meticulously designed, edited, and printed to focus exclusively on the writings and photographs of Stieglitz. O'Keeffe was determined to banish, once and for all, the other friends and influences in the conversational, contextual books by Norman and other devotees of the Stieglitz circle.

As the thirties passed, O'Keeffe began consistently to return to the desert. After 1929, O'Keeffe rarely summered at Lake George.

The White Barn, *1932, oil on board, 12" x 30"*

Stables, *1932, oil on canvas, 12" x 32"*

Barn with Snow, *1933, oil on canvas, 16" x 28"*

She sometimes visited in early spring or in late fall, her favorite season. Summer's abundant greens bored her compared to the naked branches and crisp edges that emerged as fall ended.

O'Keeffe began to collect shells in Maine, taking them back to the farmhouse and her studio at Lake George. It was more unusual to find the gently convoluted forms, many now fossilized, in New Mexico. These shells were reminders that in long-past geologic eras marine life had inhabited an ocean that was now a desert. The shell was more than an anachronism; it was another "contrarie," a riddle about life, growth, and time. From the Clam Shell and Shell and Old Shingle series of the 1920s to *Shell I* (1927, see p. 168), O'Keeffe paid attention to each shell's abstract surface features. *Shell I*, primarily in warm white and ochre hues, suggests two contrasting sculptural forms, the involuted, pear-shaped shell on its side and the spiny surrounding white coral. The same shell is upright in *Three Shells* (1937, see p. 169), seeming to face a smaller, rainbow-hued shell and a black, horn-shaped shell, both positioned on their sides before it. The possible gender symbolism—of a male shell between two females—may be a surreal message, but one lacking the textural, figural eroticism of the first single shell. *Pink Shell with Seaweed* (c. 1938, see p. 105), an enlarged spiral with softened features, is placed against a distant, hazy blue and slate landscape. This enigma seems more unified as a composition than *Three Shells*.

In *Shell on Red* (1931), the shell's edges and surface are as smooth as baby skin. The oval shell is enlarged to fill the canvas, leaving only four pure-red triangular corners as background. The desert—or the artist's brush—has eliminated time; the shell that remains is ageless. The curving pink-white shape seems alive, almost in motion, on the red ground.

Shell on Red is based on a formal design that O'Keeffe used throughout her career: the relation of the circle and triangle. The round shape could be a circle, a pie wedge (part circle, part triangle), a circumference, an extended curve, or an oval—technically an ovoid. The forms represented ranged from pure abstractions to a particular object or landscape. Kandinsky underscored the dynamic use of these forms, especially juxtaposed, saying:

The impact of an acute angle of a triangle on a circle produces an effect no less powerful than the finger of God touching the finger of Adam in Michelangelo; and fingers are not just anatomical or physiological, but something more. A triangle or a circle is something more than geometry.[12]

Circles and triangles were forms emphasized in the early books of Dow and Kandinsky. The correlation between this statement, made in 1931, and O'Keeffe's use of these forms in the same year is probably accidental.

Two oil paintings in particular, *Black and White* (1930) and *Black, Blue, and White* (1930), seem to prove his theory. Both are similar in composition: the entire ground is a curving form—a quarter circle that completely covers the canvas in three main arcs of color. This circle is bisected by an acute triangle extending diagonally from its base in the left lower and center side of the canvas toward the right upper corner. The point of interest is the triangle's tip. Both the triangle's base and the circle seem to continue beyond the canvas, a closeup technique used in previous works. *Black and White* uses black, grays, and white in a dynamic relation to each other, with the triangle primarily in white.

Black, Blue, and White is more subtle in coloration and formal design. The upper portion, left to right, melds dark gray to charcoal black to steel gray to gray. This range, with the darkest area in the center, accentuates the curving form and acts as a ground for the contrasting white triangle. The blues in the lower portion brighten the whites and grays. A thin spiral, its upper black edge merging into gray below, echoes the top ring while introducing lighter values. The next spiral is again black blending into deep charcoal in the center, with a lower edge of light charcoal.

The triangle that pierces this broad central band is two-toned —white with gray accents in diagonal brushstrokes, and charcoal with a white lower edge. The white and light charcoal areas may be seen as one two-toned triangle or as two narrow adjacent

Abstraction, *1926, oil on canvas, 30″ x 18″*

Dry Waterfall

triangles. The triangular shape is embedded in the central, deep-charcoal band. O'Keeffe's use of color for edges produces provocative contrasts.

The lower portion of the painting—the last inner circle—is most mixed in terms of color: a royal-blue–edged area becomes navy with a royal-blue inner oval. In form, the lower right corner is a continuation of the circle, but in color it echoes the white and gray tones of the triangle.

As the pointing, light double triangle pierces the widest, darkest part of the circle, its coloration is repeated in three light areas, two above and one below. Thus a muted triangle of lighter tones highlights the dark curving shapes and the central form.

The dynamic of the bisecting forms is reinforced by the complex coloration and also by the texture. Though O'Keeffe's textures are never obvious, her brushstrokes often emphasize contrasting forms. The luminous quality of the colors comes, in part, from the white sizing that shines through a few black areas in pinpoints. The circles reveal horizontal brushstrokes while the triangle carries diagonal strokes.

The triangle appears to represent O'Keeffe's "white consciousness" [13]—the mind's eye *seeing* its way through the spheres of creation, life, and earth. Whether or not meanings are attached to these forms—one could imagine a natural source of inspiration as simple as a flashlight's piercing beam in the dark—the powerful and unified composition is one of O'Keeffe's finest works of art. An inner depth is created through subtle color and shape relationships, yet the overall result is one of harmonious simplicity.

Other works incorporating the circle and triangle include the Flagpole and Leaves Series of the 1920s, *Sunset, Long Island* (1939), and *Road Past the View* (1964). One of the first abstractions of the two forms is *Line and Curve* (1927). In this work, a narrow acute triangle extends its tip to the left center edge of the canvas as the lower leg, continuing to the right center edge, bisects a quarter circle on the right. White, gray, and violet hues

Near Abiquiu, New Mexico, *1941, oil on canvas, 12" x 30"*

Long Pink Hills, *1940, oil on canvas, 7" x 18"*

create a serene, cool image. The overlapping area of the triangle base and circle creates a subtle *trompe l'oeil*.

A later painting which uses similar forms with a different result is *Ladder to the Moon* (1958). Here, a handmade wooden ladder is suspended in the sky between the night-black peak of Pedernal mountain and a half moon. The aqua-blue sky emphasizes the floating, unconnected quality of the ladder. This work is an incomplete version of Kandinsky's theory. The formal arrangements and the colors of the composition are so simple that there is no resulting dynamic or tension. The composition has occult innuendoes but overall seems more romantic than surreal. Her collage of realistic images does not produce the powerful effect of the triangle piercing the circle in *Black, Blue, and White*. It is interesting to note that her Spanish contemporary, Surrealist painter Joan Miró, combined these two approaches, creating a sign language that was "neither purely abstract nor clearly representational," according to art historian Sidra Stitch.[14] O'Keeffe, like Miró and Picasso, was undoubtedly fond of repeating geometric motifs that included circles, ovals, and triangles.

In a nonabstract painting of 1932, *Cross with Red Heart* (see p. 141), one of the group painted during one trip to the Gaspé Peninsula with Georgia Engelhard, the cross holds a pulsing three-dimensional red heart with a red tuft; this triangular heart in a white pearl circle may represent O'Keeffe's dual need to bury her love for Stieglitz (the tuft and the rooster/cock emblem atop the cross recall his pet name t.o.c.f.—the old cock's feather), and at the same time to resurrect her own heart and set it in the sky. T. S. Eliot had not yet invented the term "objective correlative" to define the concrete relation of images to inner feelings and thoughts, but the solemn yet uplifting image seems to represent a particular milestone in O'Keeffe's ongoing explorations of self-definition—by elevating her lovelorn heart, literally and figuratively, in her art, she could distance herself, even laugh at her dilemma.

Unfortunately, O'Keeffe's pure geometries from *Black Abstraction* (1927) (an impression of the last ray of consciousness as she was "etherized upon a table" for an operation on a benign breast tumor) to *Black, Blue, and White* were, for her, unwelcome reminders of the knife-edge between consciousness and unconsciousness, sanity and insanity. She did not invent forms as exquisite as these again.

The last week in December 1933 was a turning point in her recovery from her bleakest period. After the hospitalization, Bermuda, and self-imposed, listless isolation at Lake George, O'Keeffe returned to New York City on December 15 and ran into novelist Jean Toomer at An American Place. Toomer's writings had been mildly praised by Stieglitz in 1923, and he had been a guest, with Paul Rosenfeld, at Lake George in 1925. The congenial, handsome, and youthful-looking black writer was well liked in their circle of friends. He was recovering from the recent loss of his wife, and O'Keeffe spontaneously invited him to share her solitude at the Lake, so off they went. O'Keeffe's spirits perked up to such a surprising degree that Stieglitz decided, after her warm letter to him, to visit. He spent Christmas week with them, leaving three days before Toomer left.

Toomer and O'Keeffe exchanged letters over the next year as she slowly regained her urge to paint. She wrote that his presence still permeated the house, that he had given her the feeling that life was precious again, and that she was regaining her sense of balance. She missed him, and she joked that the duck she had for dinner one night missed him too. O'Keeffe affectionately described the antics of her cat, Long Tail, and the two little kittens that they had played with together. Her brief romantic attachment to Toomer faded as her health returned and she reasserted her need to follow her own course. As January rains turned to snow, O'Keeffe decided to leave for Bermuda in February. On the luxury liner cruising south, she wrote to Toomer, comparing herself to a reed being blown by the winds of her own habits. She saw no other choice for herself but to move "more and more toward a kind of aloneness—not because I wish it so but because there seems no other way."[15] Toomer responded, noting that he had gone to Taos to visit their friend Marjorie Content. In Taos,

Georgia O'Keeffe (Hands and Thimble) *by Alfred Stieglitz, 1920, photograph*

Pattern of Leaves, *1924, oil on canvas, 22⅛″ x 18⅛″*

Pink Shell with Seaweed, *c. 1938, pastel, 22" x 28"*

her two friends fell in love with each other.

In May of 1934, O'Keeffe visited Lake George without Stieglitz and then departed for New Mexico. She and Marjorie Content rented the cottage on her friend Marie Garland's ranch in Alcalde, each going her own way most of the time as they had done in Bermuda in 1932. When Jean Toomer joined them in midsummer, it was as Marjorie's fiancé, a situation that put O'Keeffe in an awkward position. She showed up unannounced and without a reservation at Arthur Pack's popular dude ranch.

Ghost Ranch was about two hours from Sante Fe by car, less by Pack's small plane. Sporting businessmen enjoyed horseback riding and other adventures at the remote wilderness retreat on the Chama River, formerly part of a Spanish land grant. Pack had a room available for one night only when O'Keeffe arrived, but she insisted on staying. She remained in residence all summer. O'Keeffe and Marjorie's two grown daughters were the witnesses at the wedding of Content and Toomer on September 1 in Taos. The couple eventually settled in Doylestown, Pennsylvania. Marjorie, a lifelong friend of Stieglitz, his brother Leopold, and Lee's daughter Elizabeth, who was her contemporary, outlived her husband and remained a friend also of Stieglitz's niece Dorothy Schubart, Elizabeth, and O'Keeffe.

That summer, O'Keeffe spent most of her time exploring the canyons and mesas in the vicinity of Ghost Ranch, painting on location for three or four days at a time before moving on to another site.

The geophysical land forms in New Mexico produced their own influence on O'Keeffe's compositions of the 1930s and 1940s. In a dissertation on this subject, scholar Jane Downer Collins has suggested how O'Keeffe systematically integrated these forms into her work:

The New Mexico landscape paintings, whether realistic or abstract, exhibit the following stylistic features, many of which were influenced by characteristics of the landscape itself:

1. *an emphasis on the configurations of the land rather than the sky which results in high horizons*
2. *an interest in ordinary and unspectacular features of the landscape*
3. *a frontal viewpoint, usually on the same level as the subject rather than high above or below, so that features of the landscape lie parallel to the picture plane and a sense of deep space is compressed*
4. *the silhouetting of forms against the sky*
5. *compositions consisting of horizontal bands of contrasting colors*
6. *a tendency to distort scale towards monumentality or to leave it ambiguous*
7. *the frequent exclusion of a middle ground and sometimes of both a foreground and middle ground so that recession into depth is kept to a minimum*
8. *a lack of interest in transient weather conditions*
9. *a preference for flat, even lighting so that forms are fully illuminated and not obscured by shadows*
10. *the suppression of individual brushstrokes to achieve a restrained, non-gestural surface except for some interplay of rough and smooth textures*
11. *the total exclusion of people, animals or anything made by man from the landscape*
12. *a respect for the wholeness of objects and consequent refusal to fragment forms*
13. *edges that are firm, but not hard*
14. *a static, motionless, timeless quality*
15. *an interest in the close-up, intimate view of single features of the landscape in addition to vistas which sometimes emphasize a correspondence between natural forms and human forms*
16. *an interest in painting fragments or details of larger forms*
17. *the minimal modeling of forms to indicate some three dimen-*

sionality but not enough to destroy a sense of two-dimensional design

18. *a tendency to simplify the appearance of the landscape by eliminating details such as trees or lines of erosion*
19. *a tendency to intensify natural colors*
20. *an attraction to sculptured, rounded, sensual shapes*
21. *the production of series of paintings of the same subject*

Collins concludes, "Paradoxically, O'Keeffe's New Mexico pictures are both realistic and abstract at the same time."[16]

Her twenty-one points add to the viewer's understanding of the principles and practices O'Keeffe developed—her own language of forms. O'Keeffe used still-life, romantic, and abstract characteristics to isolate and emphasize her subjects, giving them, as Collins points out, "a static, motionless, timeless quality." The artist's paintings of the New Mexico landscape are easily distinguishable from other work, yet also contain intentional and direct correspondences. One example already discussed is the use of similar forms in *Music—Pink and Blue* (1919), and the Pelvis Series of the 1940s. (See Chapter 3, note 15.)

O'Keeffe's artistic vision was integrally related to her life-style. She continued to be ultraselective about friendships, allowing only a few individuals, such as Anita Pollitzer and Stieglitz, to become confidantes of her innermost thoughts, and dropping anyone who no longer had anything to offer her. One friendship that lasted began when O'Keeffe met a budding concert pianist in Santa Fe in 1929. The twenty-seven-year-old Ansel Adams was on the verge of committing himself to a new career as a photographer and was in New Mexico to complete a photographic study, *Taos Pueblo,* in collaboration with writer Mary Austin.

This meeting did not develop into a lasting friendship for several years. In the meantime, Adams found painter John Marin as approachable as a country farmer, and he admired Marin's writings as well as his art.

The following year, Adams met photographer Paul Strand, whose closeup abstract realism had made a strong impression on O'Keeffe in 1917. Adams saw only Strand's negatives, but he was so inspired by their luminous quality and detail that he became more deeply committed to his own photographic career and gave up the idea of becoming a concert pianist.

Adams's work then began to receive serious acclaim at a time when photography was not yet established as a fine art. By 1933, he had already had photographic exhibitions at the Smithsonian in Washington, D.C., and the De Young Museum in San Francisco. It was time to visit gallery owners in New York, and, in particular, to meet Alfred Stieglitz. The older photographer's reputation as an artist was a major inspiration for Adams, even though his own photographic style was distinctly different. Adams believed that recognition by Stieglitz—perhaps the chance for an exhibition—would affirm his accomplishments as an artist. As Stieglitz studied the Taos portfolio and some of the Yosemite prints that Adams brought to An American Place, the two photographers became friends.

During Adams's 1933 visit to New York, O'Keeffe had become more friendly because she recognized that Adams was a good craftsman. She was instrumental in introducing Adams to an ardent photography enthusiast, David Hunter McAlpin, whom she had met in 1928 at a dinner party in her honor. McAlpin later told O'Keeffe about Ghost Ranch, for owner Arthur Pack was his friend from Princeton and a business colleague. McAlpin had begun his collection of drawings and prints in college. His faculty adviser at Princeton, Professor Clifton R. Hall, taught American history, but his personal special interest was art history—the paintings, drawings, and artists of each era. McAlpin became a businessman, photographer, and one of the first collectors of Stieglitz's photographs. One of McAlpin's favorite prints was of O'Keeffe's hands with a sewing thimble (see p. 103).[17] In this famous portrait, the rough skin of O'Keeffe's fingers contrasts with their graceful diagonal curves and the dark, soft cloth she appears to stitch.

Katchina, *1936, oil on canvas, 7" x 7"*

Beauford Delaney, c. 1940, pastel, 20" x 15"

One day in 1933, O'Keeffe called McAlpin and invited him to a Russian film being shown at Union Square. Adams, by coincidence, had gone to the same movie, and she introduced them. This meeting led to a lasting friendship between Adams and McAlpin and to two memorable photography outings in 1937 and 1938. In 1940 McAlpin became the initial chairman of the first Department of Photography at the Museum of Modern Art.

Adams was a fervent admirer of Stieglitz, but he was not comfortable with the precious quality of his circle of artists. Adams's F.16 group in California, including Imogen Cunningham and Edward Weston, had dispersed as soon as their first exhibition made its aesthetic statement. Edward Steichen's soft-focus images were too sentimental for Adams, now a convert to hard-edged realism; he had not seen Steichen's recent portraits for *Vogue*.

Adams recalled, in a personal interview, that he made many visits to An American Place and saw O'Keeffe, Dove, Marin, and Dorothy Norman. "I saw a lot of Marsden Hartley," Adams remembered:

Some afternoons, about 4 o'clock, he'd say, "Let's go out to the Met [museum] to look at the Stieglitz pictures." So we'd go out there, and go downstairs to the basement where they kept the prints in a baggage cart, and he'd go right to them and pick out the portrait of him that Stieglitz did and look at it. Meanwhile, I'd be poring through the others, trying to see them all, when he'd say, "I've got to go now; I just wanted to check on it."[18]

Adams returned to the West Coast and continued to earn his living as a commercial photographer. His work had, by that time, been featured in other exhibitions, including shows at the Albright Knox Gallery in Buffalo, Yale University Art Gallery in New Haven, and the De Young Museum in San Francisco in 1934 and 1935. Adams still wanted, above all, the sponsorship of Stieglitz. In May 1935, he wrote to Stieglitz that the visits to An American Place were the high point of his experiences in art.

In January of 1936, Stieglitz decided to give Adams an exhibition at An American Place. The exceptional technical, aesthetic, and humanitarian qualities of forty-five Adams prints have earned them a lasting place in the history of photography.[19] Adams had the eye of an artist, and the prints also were proofs of the fine processing methods he was busy perfecting.

O'Keeffe spent part of each year in New York, and she helped hang Adams's show, but she spent as little time as possible at the Place. In 1935, she had been at Ghost Ranch from June through November. She was staying in the adobe house about a half mile down a deserted road from the main ranch, and it felt more like home than any place she had ever lived. She began to make improvements in and around the house and thought about installing large picture windows that would give her a better view of the cliffs from inside her studio. The dwelling's isolated location and roomy studio and living quarters suited her needs perfectly, even providing the space for occasional houseguests. She propped a ladder against the side of the house so that she could climb onto the flat roof each evening to view the spectacular sunsets that illuminated the imposing view in all directions.

Her house was out of sight of the main ranch, down a winding dirt road, on a flat stretch of red desert spotted with cactus, prickly pears, and sagebrush. Because distance is relative and difficult to judge in the desert, the house seemed closer to imposing views in both directions—the blue-appearing Pedernal Mountain to the east and the ochre, orange, and red cliffs to the west. O'Keeffe often painted both views as close as they appeared to be.

In one notably personal painting, *The House Where I Live* (1937)—first given the more casual title *House I Live In*—the long, narrow adobe house is painted in a horizontal view with Pedernal's blue, truncated cone-shaped peak rising behind it. The mountain, more than five miles away, is actually covered with dark green pines and deciduous trees—the blue color is an illusion created by the bright desert sun, the distortions of distance, and O'Keeffe's imagination.

Ghost Ranch, *1948, photograph by Philippe Halsman. Copyright Philippe Halsman*

Dark Mesa and Pink Sky, *1930, oil on canvas, 16" x 29⅞"*

Purple Hills Near Abiquiu, *1935, oil on canvas, 16⅛" x 30⅛"*

On the other side of her house is a canyon surrounded by a semicircular cliff face about one hundred feet high, with a chimney-shaped cliff at one end. Layers of white, yellow, ochre, orange, and red rock indicate Precambrian granites from the Summerville, Morrison, and Dakota periods, dating back to the first geologic age, the Paleozoic Era. The land's awe-inspiring old age was transformed into agelessness before the original eye of O'Keeffe. At dawn and dusk, the cliffs' towering rainbow colors extend to touch the sky. For O'Keeffe, the sunsets were beautiful to watch but too sentimental to paint; the sky would always be her versions of robin's egg blue, sky blue, eternal blue.

Nearby, a series of hills continues the color spectrum to blood red, magenta, violet, and green—green stone, clay, and earth. The natural hues of the water-starved, now barren landscape and the odd, appealing forms of the cliffs, hills, mountains, and wind-bent, dried out trunks of trees expressed truth and universal beauty to O'Keeffe. Whereas Stieglitz had centered his search for truth in portraits, clouds, and buildings, O'Keeffe had chosen a desert, unpopulated except for rattlesnakes, scorpions, a few hawks, small birds, and the cats, dogs, and livestock belonging to the Spanish-Indian inhabitants of the nearby town of Abiquiu.

Her exhibition of 1936 at An American Place was an even greater critical success than her triumph a decade earlier when *Black Iris* and other large close-ups had created a sensation. O'Keeffe had regained her sense of humor enough to be amused by Lewis Mumford's review in *The New Yorker,* even though he was still psychoanalyzing her enigmatic style. In the January 18, 1936, issue, Mumford noted:

Mid the throng of good shows that have opened the new year, that of Georgia O'Keeffe at An American place stands out . . . every painting is a chapter in her autobiography, and yet the revelation

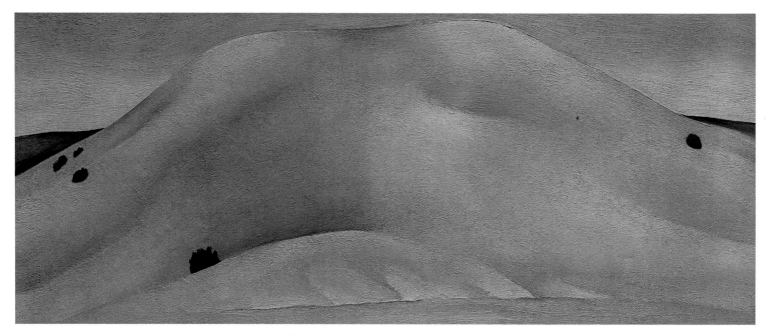

Soft Gray, Alcalde Hill, *1929–1930, oil on canvas, 10⅛″ x 24⅛″*

is so cunningly made that it probably eludes her own conscious appraisal. As soon as one realizes that she is neither a botanist who looks at flowers through a magnifying glass nor a comparative anatomist who collects the skulls of the North American desert fauna, one is brought face to face with the real problem. What has she lived through? And what do these turkey feathers and bare hills and bleached bones convey in terms of one's own experience? . . .

The present show brings, for O'Keeffe's admirers, a resurgence of life and a resurrection of spirit. The epitome of the whole show is the painting of the ram's head, with its horns acting like wings, lifted up against the gray, wind-swept clouds; at its side is a white hollyhock flower. In conception and execution this is one of the most brilliant paintings O'Keeffe has done. Not only is it a piece of consummate craftsmanship, but it likewise possesses that mysterious force, that hold upon the hidden soul, which distinguishes important communication from the casual reports of the eye . . . O'Keeffe uses themes and juxtapositions no less unexpected than those of the Surrealists, but she uses them in a fashion that makes them seem inevitable and natural, grave and beautiful.

In September of 1936, conductor Leopold Stokowski was among the guests at Arthur Pack's Ghost Ranch, and he was among the famous elite—including Alexander Calder, Albert Einstein, Louise Nevelson, Calvin Klein, Scott Momaday, and Allen Ginsberg—who would express an admiration for O'Keeffe's art.

In October, O'Keeffe changed her New York City residence to a penthouse at 405 East 54th Street, complaining that the service at the Shelton was unsatisfactory. By February 1937, O'Keeffe had completed her largest flower painting to date. The four lush, giant-sized jimson blooms in stages of unfolding were unveiled at a party at Elizabeth Arden's plush salon. O'Keeffe, the guest of honor, looked grim and pale as she stood beside her sophisticated contemporary, Arden. Although they used paint in different ways, O'Keeffe and Arden respected each other and enjoyed each

Chimney Cliffs with Red Hills

other's company. The following month, O'Keeffe visited her so-cialite sister Anita, who had moved from Providence to a mansion on Ocean Boulevard in Palm Beach. Anita devised a plan to fill the spacious downstairs rooms and long corridors with the paintings by her sister that she had begun to collect. O'Keeffe returned to New York in June, but she was annoyed that Dorothy Norman was visiting Stieglitz daily at the Place, taking notes as he recounted his past—from early experiments with photography and photogra-phy publications to dreams about flying and death. O'Keeffe went to Lake George with Stieglitz in late June. Stieglitz enjoyed medi-tative discussions with Swami Nikhilananda and a visit from Har-old Clurman and Elia Kazan. O'Keeffe departed for Ghost Ranch in July and remained there until December.

One high point of 1937 was a trip O'Keeffe took with Ansel Adams and Dave McAlpin through Arizona and New Mexico. Their small party met at Ghost Ranch. O'Keeffe drove her Ford and the others drove in a station wagon packed with supplies. The head wrangler at Ghost Ranch, Orville Cox, came along as a guide. Since he was one-eighth Indian and a native of the area, he could interpret the dialects as the group journeyed through Canyon de Chelly, Durango, and a few other places. The most dangerous mo-ment of the trip came when a storm turned the dirt roads with wide arroyos into almost-unnavigable terrain, but the hardy trav-elers made it through the worst spots, joking later about the mud-spattered cars.

In September 1938, the three joined McAlpin's business part-ner, Godfrey Rockefeller, and his wife for a seventeen-day pack trip in the high country. They met at Adams's house in Yosemite. Adams wrote to Stieglitz that O'Keeffe's presence on the trip in-spired him to photograph Yosemite all over again. Adams took two white mules loaded with photographic equipment: two pan-niers for his four-by-five camera, a small Iconta, a tripod, and other equipment. The group traveled east of Yosemite from the Lyell Fork of the Merced River Basin. They camped for three to four days at Cathedral Lake and then moved to the stream below

Rogers and Electra mountains. The weather was perfect, and, when they reached sites at ten thousand feet, quite cold.

O'Keeffe did sketching on both trips. McAlpin and Adams took pictures. For Christmas in 1938, Adams made albums of about forty 8-by-10-inch prints from the trip and sent an album to each group member. O'Keeffe and Stieglitz were both delighted that the prints captured the unspoiled splendor of the high country.

The photographs that Adams took on the two outings show a relaxed side of O'Keeffe that no other photographer, including Stieglitz, had yet recorded. In a 1937 photograph taken at Ghost Ranch, O'Keeffe's profile is quite close to the border of a painting, *Gerald's Tree*. She is setting it against her car in preparation for painting on location. Her curving form and the creases in her shirt and jeans echo the forms of the dead tree and creased hills in the painting. In the foreground, light falls on a rectangular box with brushes and a palette that appears pale and empty in relation to the rectangle of the canvas just above it. These two rectangles and O'Keeffe's profile are all viewed in diagonal lines in Adams's por-trait. As artful as the framing of the images appears to be, it was unposed. Adams had tracked O'Keeffe to the spot where she was painting on location. "I trailed her down," Adams recalled. "She said, 'What are you doing here?' I said, 'I'm going to take a pho-tograph of you in the station wagon.' She laughed, 'I'm not going to stop painting for you.' I said 'Perfect.'"[20]

In another memorable profile, O'Keeffe has a small sketch pad on her knees and is seated at the edge of a canyon looking down. O'Keeffe's dark profile and the dark ovoid of the inner canyon appear to mirror each other. The photograph speaks volumes about her immovable nature and lasting attraction to nature forms. These and other images remain a tribute to the friendship of Adams and O'Keeffe.

As O'Keeffe and Stieglitz exchanged news with Adams and his wife Virginia, Adams urged them to allow O'Keeffe's paintings to be exhibited in San Francisco and on the West Coast. Although Stieglitz had been featuring her work in annual exhibitions, he had not allowed the paintings to be shown outside of the eastern cities.

Stieglitz wrote to O'Keeffe that he had moved out of their apartment and back to the Shelton, which was closer to his gallery. He moved back and forth over the next year, preferring the Shelton's full hotel service when O'Keeffe was away. In 1938, he suffered a coronary illness and pneumonia and required first a nurse and then a housekeeper to look after him while O'Keeffe was at Ghost Ranch. When she returned to New York in late October, her paintings lacked the "resurgence of life" her work had contained in 1936.

As usual, O'Keeffe hung her own exhibition of January 1939 at

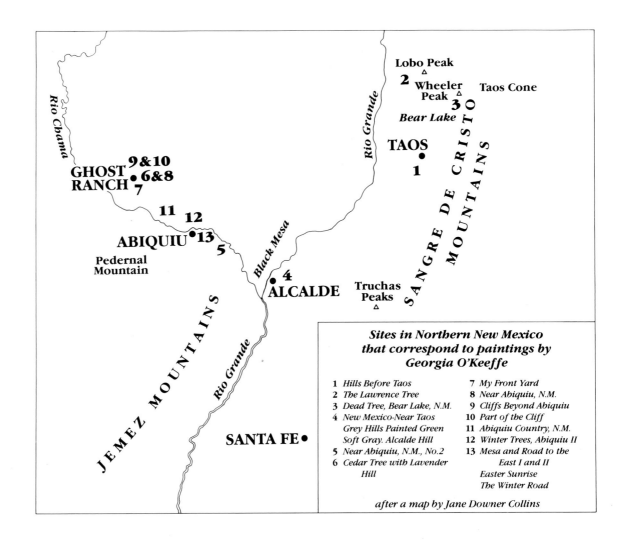

Sites in Northern New Mexico that correspond to paintings by Georgia O'Keeffe

1 *Hills Before Taos*
2 *The Lawrence Tree*
3 *Dead Tree, Bear Lake, N.M.*
4 *New Mexico-Near Taos Grey Hills Painted Green Soft Gray. Alcalde Hill*
5 *Near Abiquiu, N.M., No.2*
6 *Cedar Tree with Lavender Hill*
7 *My Front Yard*
8 *Near Abiquiu, N.M.*
9 *Cliffs Beyond Abiquiu*
10 *Part of the Cliff*
11 *Abiquiu Country, N.M.*
12 *Winter Trees, Abiquiu II*
13 *Mesa and Road to the East I and II Easter Sunrise The Winter Road*

after a map by Jane Downer Collins

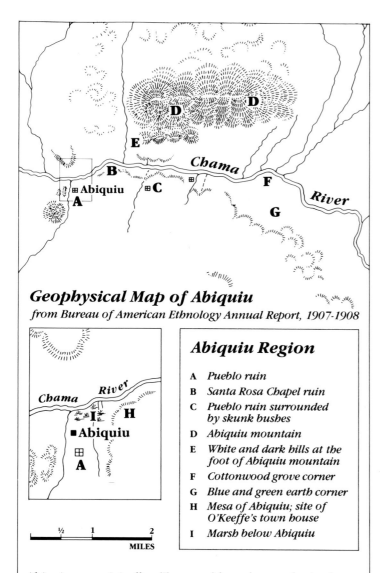

Geophysical Map of Abiquiu
from Bureau of American Ethnology Annual Report, 1907-1908

Abiquiu Region

A *Pueblo ruin*
B *Santa Rosa Chapel ruin*
C *Pueblo ruin surrounded by skunk bushes*
D *Abiquiu mountain*
E *White and dark hills at the foot of Abiquiu mountain*
F *Cottonwood grove corner*
G *Blue and green earth corner*
H *Mesa of Abiquiu; site of O'Keeffe's town house*
I *Marsh below Abiquiu*

Abiquiu was originally a Tewa pueblo and was colonized by the Spaniards and a number of Hopi captives in the nineteenth century. In the early 1900s Abiquiu was a Spanish-speaking community of Spanish-Indians. It currently includes a Moslem population and a few white inhabitants.

The Place. She was moody and showed signs of being edgy regarding an expense-paid trip to Hawaii for Dole Pineapple Company. Dole expected O'Keeffe to give them one painting of a pineapple that could be used in their advertising, so the commission seemed almost like a free two-month vacation. McAlpin and Stieglitz urged her to go. Although O'Keeffe later told at least one friend that the trip was one of her favorite times, there is other evidence to the contrary. When O'Keeffe landed in Honolulu, she dismissed the notion of painting near her hotel, as Dole officials expected. She packed her painting supplies and searched out remote parts of the islands, finding waterfalls and exotic, brightly colored flowers to paint. Her images of the island's unusual flowers in shrill colors and the somber, rigid, and cold paintings of waterfalls were not critical successes. Dole officials, consternated that, at their expense, she had refused to paint a single pineapple, had a pineapple tree in bud flown to her New York penthouse. When she finished the pineapple painting, her haggard expression as she posed, in her usual black dress, beside the painting, possibly foreshadowed a nervous breakdown.

Her physical and mental condition and her confinement were closely guarded secrets. Just as she had experienced mysterious depressions in the late twenties when Stieglitz was also unwell and in the early thirties, her current condition was probably psychosomatic.

The 1940s brought a widening gap between the times O'Keeffe and Stieglitz spent living together. She arranged for a young girl to live in and take care of him while she went to Bermuda for her own recovery. Although she wrote to friends that she enjoyed the sun and the company of young people, the social set in Bermuda found O'Keeffe to be too peculiar and demanding for their tastes. Somehow, without realizing it, O'Keeffe spoiled the easygoing moods of the others. In June she was back at Ghost Ranch, finalizing her plans to purchase the property from Arthur Pack and assuming ownership on October 30.

Stieglitz spent part of each summer at Lake George, but his

severe angina made it necessary for him to limit his activity to correspondence and short walks. Despite his illness, The Place had its annual openings. Dorothy Norman was still managing business matters, but she sometimes sent her secretaries to help Stieglitz instead of coming herself. She was actively pursuing projects spanning mythology, literature, philosophy, and world peace. With seemingly boundless energy in 1938, she founded and edited a literary/cultural periodical titled *Twice a Year*. In the harsh years leading to the Second World War, her goal was to feature socially relevant ideas. Despite growing evidence of atrocities in Germany, Stieglitz refused to take a political stand. Gradually, his apolitical attitude, his intransigence about new art trends, and his increasing physical debility isolated him more and more from his former friends, including Norman. Yet she silently supported his wish to remain "on duty" at his gallery the last few years of his life, even though visitors were infrequent. Stieglitz wrote her into his will but O'Keeffe saw to it that the will was changed so that she would be omitted except in the unlikely case that O'Keeffe would die before Stieglitz.

Stieglitz may have been in poor health, but he continued to worry about O'Keeffe. He wrote to friends that she was in pain and not painting much. In 1941, she spent five months at Ghost Ranch. She also had her eye on a deserted Catholic mission in the tiny town of Abiquiu. It looked perfect for winter quarters. The compound was surrounded by a cracking adobe wall. In the center of the rectangular building was a patio with an intriguing door.

Abiquiu, built on a mesa overlooking the Chama River, was originally a Tewa Indian village, situated between the sacred Pedernal Mountain and two high mesas. The influx of Spanish settlers from Mexico in the nineteenth century brought the Spanish language, the crucifix, and accompanying flocks of Catholic missionaries and priests. Since the town had no commerce, no material

wealth, nothing of value, the church had abandoned its adobe mission in the 1930s. The simple town church eventually lost its full-time priest and settled for a traveling priest. The only white settlers were a family who ran a general store below the mesa on the one-lane dirt road that curved through the hills between Española and Alcalde. The entire state of New Mexico was still undeveloped by twentieth-century standards, and the state legislators often spoke Spanish rather than English.

Abiquiu was one of the state's most remote outposts. Spanish was the only language in common use, and there was no reason for outsiders to visit. The community of less than one hundred individuals of mixed Spanish and Indian heritage had no idea why Georgia O'Keeffe wanted to move into their neighborhood. Yet O'Keeffe persisted until she convinced the Catholic church to sell the deserted property in 1945.

O'Keeffe helped to put the town on the map. In the 1970s, after her fame was widespread, she agreed to the idea of preserving her house as a historic landmark. Congress passed a bill to create the Georgia O'Keeffe National Historic Site in 1980, allocating funds for the perpetual upkeep of her house and tasteful preservation of the site. The National Park Service released an environmental assessment of the plan in May 1982, finding "no significant impact" on land, endangered species, and wetlands management with minimal negative impacts on the cultural resources of Abiquiu. But by 1983, O'Keeffe reversed herself and requested that Congress rescind its decision, saying that the neighbors would be inconvenienced if her house became a tourist attraction. Just as Stieglitz had been ousted from the Camera Club and had fought for reinstatement in order to promptly resign, O'Keeffe never would be comfortable until she was assured that she had the upper hand in her dealings with institutions.[21]

Mule's Skull with Pink Poinsettias, *1937, oil on canvas, 40" x 30"*

5. Bone Vision

Among O'Keeffe's famous creations of the 1940s were the Pelvis Series, close-ups of a cow's pelvic girdle with the blue sky appearing inside the bone's ovoid hollow—"the bones and the blue," as she called it. She painted the red hills, the cliffs, and other favorite spots. A "black place" looked like endless elephant hides, and a "white place" with truncated conical columns of ash-white rock looked like nature's own Grecian ruins. Why did O'Keeffe paint these particular images and choose to live in this particular setting? Beaumont Newhall has speculated that an unconscious drive compelled her, as an artist, to move to the Southwest:

One key to that—this may sound oversimplified and meaningless: intuition plays an important part. My wife [Christy Newhall] calls it the inner truth magnet—the unconscious drive. It doesn't matter if the name is Stieglitz or O'Keeffe—or that they're not aware of the accumulation of impressions stored away in the unconscious. We've got psychological studies that there is some drive that forces the artist to carry on, and only later is the intuitive product recognized. Germans call it Formwollen *or the "will to form"—I cannot will it, but it is willed. This is related in the writings of the Viennese art historian Alois Riegl, who argued successfully that art shapes technique—that in the desire of the artist to express, he will make breakthroughs in technique . . . Another way to say it is that inspiration is grounded in an artist's unconscious. The word is dangerous because it's used so often by psychoanalysts. There is an absolute* drive *for the truly creative artist. O'Keeffe was driven to the Southwest. She didn't leave Stieglitz for the usual reasons.*

O'Keeffe's formative experiences seem to fit Newhall's theory about the "inner truth magnet." Her early memories—the fine, soft dirt in Sun Prairie, her mother's reading of Wild West stories, the "beckoning" Blue Ridge Mountains at Chatham, and long walks across the desert and Palo Duro canyon in Texas—all had culminated in her move to New Mexico. The dramatically colored and shaped formations of Palo Duro Canyon have an uncanny similarity to the canyon formations near Abiquiu. At each of these previous sites, O'Keeffe had made significant breakthroughs in her art. At each turning point, she also had, consciously or subconsciously, made the decision to leave a close friend behind in order to move on.

As in the past, O'Keeffe's decision to maintain her artistic independence from Stieglitz had social repercussions. When Adams wrote to McAlpin on February 3, 1941, he expressed concern not about the art of their two close friends but about their estrangement from others. Adams feared that their "strange intellectual feudalism" was out of step with the times and was alienating the two from other artists and the ever-changing world. In the six-page letter, Adams again expressed the depth of his regard for Stieglitz and O'Keeffe. Adams, as a humanist, rejected the "negative world" they lived in. He had to put up with the complaints of San Francisco friends who wanted to purchase and exhibit O'Keeffe's art but had been rebuffed.

Adams recalled, "He [Stieglitz] was very demanding, rather possessive, and super-protective. He had a lot of showmanship, in a way, but I know that he was sincere. He felt that because a person had a lot of money and could buy anything he wanted, it might not mean anything to him. I know what he was seeking—understanding."

Newhall, likewise, noted of Stieglitz, "He was very much alone at the end. There is a long record of disillusionments, misunderstandings, and loss of friends, because Stieglitz was an absolute dictator. It was *his way* that led to the success of Photo-Secession Gallery. He was a very domineering man." O'Keeffe, like Stieglitz, was used to getting her own way. She became more domineering during this period. Stieglitz was frail, and the two were living further apart. O'Keeffe realized that someday soon the responsibility for her art, Stieglitz's photographs, and the numerous works that had entered Stieglitz's galleries, now overcrowding the storage vaults—all of the art and all of the responsibility—would be hers.

Adams remained a concerned friend of each, absorbing some of the tension created by their personal differences and aloofness toward others. In 1945, he wrote to McAlpin, outlining his idea of forming a trust to keep the Stieglitz collection of art, photographs, sculptures, and documents intact. Adams explained, "I knew there were problems. I could see that there was no record at all. I didn't know what would happen, but I guessed. You have to have everything accounted for, everything inventoried, as they say. But there was no paperwork at all." The artists just brought their artworks and left them at the gallery. Stieglitz considered himself a caretaker since he never took a commission from the sale of a painting. Since there were no registration papers at the time of Stieglitz's death, the IRS called in witnesses who successfully argued that the works did belong to the artists. While the artists' testimony released the estate from an enormous tax burden, most of these works were, in fact, part of the Stieglitz Collection. The proof of ownership was used both ways.

Adams talked to O'Keeffe only once about the idea of setting up a trust fund. The idea was dropped. "I think she was worried, too," he recalled. "She said to me one time, 'It's a very perplexing business.' She was working there [at An American Place] one time, doing little artistic things. O'Keeffe didn't participate as much as she did in the early days."

O'Keeffe was shopping in Española, the town closest to Abiquiu, when she received a telegram that Stieglitz was seriously ill. Without changing her work clothes, she drove directly to Albuquerque and took the next plane to New York. O'Keeffe was at his bedside when Stieglitz died on July 13, 1946, at 1:30 A.M.

She remained in New York but was reluctant to see most of the friends who came to pay their respects. Dave McAlpin, Adams, art connoisseur Carl Van Vechten, and one or two others were welcome. McAlpin lunched with O'Keeffe on July 19. She was coping with Stieglitz's death with a new serenity and calm. She maintained her usual exclusivity and her strict habit of keeping her feelings to herself, yet she did admit to Adams that the world seemed strange without Stieglitz.

Beaumont Newhall's account of Stieglitz's death—in dreams and reality—gives one insider's view of his last days: "Stieglitz told me—two ways he wanted to die: the first, seated in his studio on a stool holding up to the skylight the perfect glass negative; then he would slump on the floor and the negative would smash to a hundred pieces. The other way would be to hire a plane and be driven up and up until the very altitude took his breath away.

"We [Newhall and his first wife, Nancy] dropped in the Saturday before the Wednesday he died just to see him, say hello. And we found him alone, lying down. Then in came a girl who was looking after him, living in the apartment while O'Keeffe was away. He'd had a heart attack, and the doctor had come and given him some morphine. He was perfectly conscious, and we talked for about twenty minutes. The girl came back, and we left. The next thing we heard was that his two friends, Zoler and Jerome Melquist, came in, and they took him back to his apartment. He never went back to American Place."

No memorial service or wake was held, but relatives and friends of the deceased gathered on Sunday morning, July 14, in the main chapel at Campbell's Funeral Home at Eighty-first Street and Madison Avenue. The closed coffin was at the altar at the end of the room. By 11:00 A.M., many of the rows were filled with people waiting for their turn to walk past the coffin. Some family members clustered together. As recalled by Lowe, Georgia O'Keeffe showed "calm dignity, her self-containment making the extravagant tears and sobbing embraces of some around her seem grotesque."[1] Around noon, the crowds began to disperse onto the sidewalk. O'Keeffe climbed into the waiting limousine that took her behind the hearse to the crematorium in Queens.

There is no account that the will was read before the relatives of the deceased, as is usually the case. As one relative noted, Stieglitz had never cared much about wills and property. He had accepted art from others as an act of absolute faith rather than ownership. Stieglitz's only request was that his remains be cremated and his ashes sprinkled around a huge pine tree at Lake George.

O'Keeffe took the ashes up to Lake George with Dave McAlpin. McAlpin's wife Sally, painter Charles Sheeler, and his wife Musya followed in another car. En route, the party stopped on a bank above the road for a lunch of leg of lamb. Then McAlpin drove O'Keeffe to the Stieglitz property while the others headed for the McAlpins' summer house on Hewitt Lake. At Lake George, O'Keeffe took the urn and was gone for about forty-five minutes. She remained at the lake as McAlpin headed north to rejoin his party. O'Keeffe, by this time, had severed or cooled her relations with most of the Stieglitz family members. O'Keeffe left Lake George, the site of her formative years as a professional artist. Although she maintained warm contact with Elizabeth and Dorothy Schubart, her relations with the rest of the family had already been severed. Now the Stieglitz circle chapter of her life was nearly over.

O'Keeffe made the decision to deposit the Stieglitz letters and papers, some of which were under Norman's care through her association with Stieglitz, at Yale University. There Donald Gallup, curator of American Literature, began to supervise the cataloguing of the vast collection. Graduate student Peter Bunnell was later hired to solicit additional documents.[2]

Under the provisions of Stieglitz's will, dated June 25, 1937, and amended on February 4, 1942, Stieglitz bequeathed all of his property, real and personal, to Georgia O'Keeffe, giving her the power to utilize his estate in her lifetime, to maintain herself in comfort, and to pass on her control in any way she chose to designate in her own will.

O'Keeffe began a task that would have been a major undertaking even for an institution, let alone one individual. Fully involved with the administrative details of settling the estate, she first consulted with Carl Van Vechten about the disposition of the valuable prints, drawings, photographs, paintings, and sculpture that Stieglitz had amassed throughout his lifetime. She sent away the other friends who offered a helping hand. Ironically, Stieglitz's blood relatives were excluded from any consideration, even

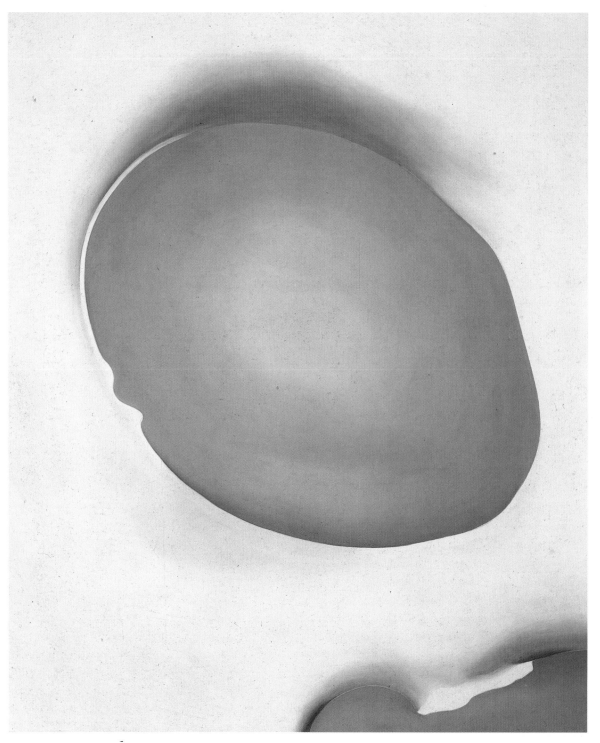

Pelvis I (Pelvis with Blue), *1944, oil on canvas, 36″ x 30″*

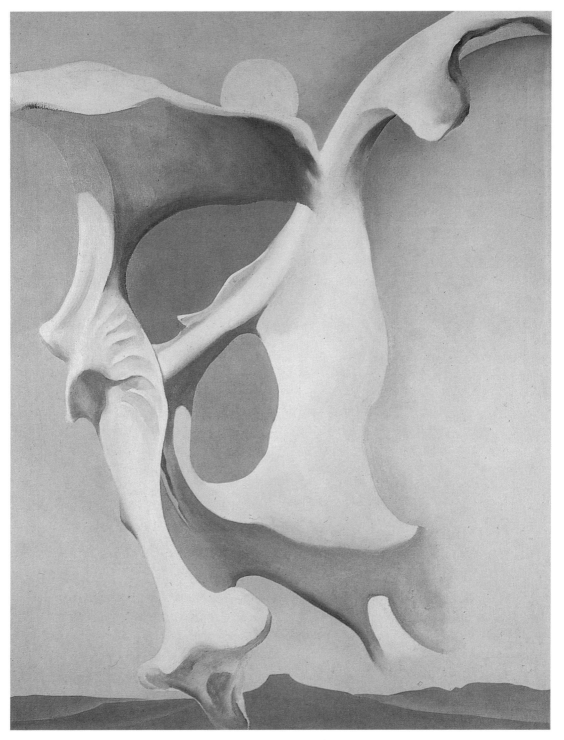

Pelvis with Moon, *1943, oil on canvas, 30" x 24"*

though O'Keeffe and Stieglitz had survived their first years together by living in the homes of his brother Leopold in the winter and his mother Hedwig in the summer, also using the modest trust from his father and living allowances from his family to make ends meet. Without a thought about owing anything to the Stieglitz family, O'Keeffe remained determined to control, almost singlehandedly, Stieglitz's lifelong art collection.

O'Keeffe would not admit her mixed feelings over Stieglitz's death. Their conflicts had created an unremitting, relentless animosity and tension by 1929, according to one friend. While O'Keeffe had willingly assumed primary responsibility for Stieglitz's support and care, she had begun to loathe New York and resented being expected to be there for any length of time.

At An American Place, Dorothy Norman's proprietorship was anathema to O'Keeffe. She never accepted Norman's supportive position of championing Stieglitz's talents as a photographer and impresario of modern art. His warm regard for Norman's budding talents as a writer, editor, and photographer made O'Keeffe livid. O'Keeffe, as her marriage foundered, may have blamed Norman for the conflicts that had ravaged her relations with Stieglitz. O'Keeffe admitted that she was lonely, but her mood was pleasant and calm. She could both relax and work hard; most important, she could set her own pace and direction.

As she sorted through the collection, she found the original prints by Adams that Stieglitz had exhibited in 1936, and she wrote to Adams about them. He replied on September 6, 1946, that the prints had "nostalgic quality" that distinguished them from other photographs. He suggested that she give them to Dave McAlpin, the Newhalls, filmmaker Henwar Rodakiewicz, John Marin, Dorothy Norman, and Andrew Dasburg. He offered O'Keeffe first choice if she wanted one.

After the Stieglitz Collection, as it came to be known, was documented, primarily by O'Keeffe and her assistant, Doris Bry, she announced that most of the art would go to five major museums: the National Gallery of Art in Washington, D.C., the Metropolitan

Museum in New York, the Art Institute of Chicago, Fisk University in Nashville, and the San Francisco Museum of Art. The first three museums received proportionally more and qualitatively better works, with the National Gallery's portion including the most complete set of prints of Alfred Stieglitz's photographs. The Boston Museum of Fine Arts, the Philadelphia Museum of Art, and the International Museum of Photography at the George Eastman House, Rochester, New York, also received some works.

Van Vechten's involvement with Fisk University had influenced O'Keeffe's decision to send works there. The museums chosen were in different cities and states, and, on the surface, would make the collection available to a diverse public. However, a string of stipulations concerning care, reproduction rights, and exhibitions accompanied each gift. As a result of these stringent rules, exhibitions of the collection were severely limited, and none of Stieglitz's photographs at these museums were accessible, by normal means, for thirty or more years. O'Keeffe agreed to an exhibition of the photographs at the National Gallery in 1958, on the condition that she would have exclusive control of the arrangements and catalogue. In the late 1970s, the master set of photographs at the National Gallery was catalogued over a period of about five years by Kress fellow Sarah Greenough, who conceived and supervised the opening of the Stieglitz retrospective exhibition there on February 3, 1983.

O'Keeffe's virtual paranoia concerning the care, use, and availability of the works was based, in part, on her mistrust of institutions, but also, in part, on her own version of the exclusivity she had learned from Stieglitz. Ironically, she was so concerned about the legal, rather than the spiritual, terms that she, in effect, sealed off access to the materials she was dispersing. This seems contradictory to Stieglitz's intent as well as to his act of giving three collections of photographs—his own and others—to William Ivins, curator of the print collection at the Metropolitan Museum, as unrestricted gifts in 1923, 1928, and 1933.

Before giving up her permanent residence in New York and

moving back to New Mexico, O'Keeffe painted *The Brooklyn Bridge*. The Stieglitz Collection contained an evocative etching by John Marin, also titled *Brooklyn Bridge* (1913), which might have stirred her sensibilities. As Marin's swaying bridge and New York skyline catapult into one moving mass, the city's frenetic energy comes alive. Unfortunately, O'Keeffe's painting was rigid and cold, without a trace of Marin's linear thrust and elasticity. Perhaps O'Keeffe's frozen view characterized her changing relations with New York, for it was her last city painting.

Back in Abiquiu she was busy rebuilding the house that she had finally wrested from the control of the Catholic church. The building and site had three main attractions missing at Ghost Ranch. Originally, she had been drawn to the deserted building's wooden door, leading to a patio. O'Keeffe often talked of buying the property because of that door, which she felt led to a place of peace and spiritual solace. The second attraction was the wall surrounding the house and land, assuring privacy. The third was a large plot of land with water rights—perfect for a garden. O'Keeffe told friends that she was tired of eating canned fruits and vegetables. With the help of a local handyman, Frank Martinez, and his wife Dorothea, who became her housekeeper and cook, she planted an extensive garden, starting with apple trees and vegetables, then expanding the varieties and introducing exotic flowers. She installed an irrigation system of interconnecting canals to water her plants. The old adobe was cracking, and she admired the work of the village women as they repaired the walls by hand, inside and out, with red clay. She turned one back room into a vault for her paintings.

The house behind the long wall looks down from the crest of the mesa onto a dirt road that winds in an **S**-shaped curve past the town and west toward Ghost Ranch, about twenty miles away. Although O'Keeffe was surrounded by a Spanish-speaking population, she never learned Spanish. Unlike Stieglitz and others in his circle who were fluent in German and French, O'Keeffe, who had studied no languages, was more typical of midwesterners who stuck to English, whether at home or abroad. The new house was perfect for guests and also had a painting studio. O'Keeffe wrote to Adams in 1950 and in 1951, inviting him to come for a visit. He and his wife Virginia did drop in in late April of 1951. She visited them in San Francisco that year and accompanied them to the De Young Museum for an exhibition of "Japanese wrap-around things," according to Adams.

Both her letters and accounts from friends indicate that O'Keeffe's artistic output suffered in the fifties. In the twenties, despite the discomfort of putting up with many strong personalities and frivolous social demands, nosy people, and the media, she had been innovative and productive. Now, in her sixties, she finally had control of her own life. She was finally alone.

New York painter Robert Dash was a student at the University of New Mexico when he first met O'Keeffe in the fifties. In an interview at his Long Island studio on July 25, 1979, he shared his vivid memories of getting to know O'Keeffe. Dash's contact with O'Keeffe was typical of her associations with younger people with artistic interests who found their way to Ghost Ranch.

Dash began, "I think I met her in 1952 in the Student Union building at the University of New Mexico early in the morning. We had a cup of coffee. I knew her then-secretary Betty Pilkington slightly. Later I got to know her better. Miss O'Keeffe was en route to Mexico on a trip with Sandy Calder. Betty, who was in one of my classes, introduced me to her. We chatted maybe ten minutes." In 1953, Betty was working more regularly for O'Keeffe, and Dash began to spend his weekends visiting Betty at O'Keeffe's house in Abiquiu.

Dash pointed out,

My first real recollection of her was that she was entirely fascinating and someone to be studied. She walks better than anyone else I've ever seen, and she uses the English language in the best of all possible ways—at its simplest and most direct. She was always saying, "Isn't that good?" "Isn't that bad?" "That is nice." "All

Winter Trees III, *1953, oil on canvas, 36" x 30"*

Grey Tree by the Road, *1952, oil on canvas, 16" x 20"*

right. It is hot." She didn't care much for amplification. In the desert, it doesn't seem to be necessary.

Apparently, I did very little talking because she said to Betty, "He's always studying me; he makes me nervous," which was not my intention. She was making me more nervous, and I had a feeling that at any moment she might strike, which sometimes proved true.

For example, we were staying at the Ghost Ranch. It was at breakfast. Georgia was grumbling, "People say I whirl rattlesnakes around my head. I don't." And she opened the door and said, "There's one now." And she said, "SHOO!! SHOO!!" and that snake took off.

I was witness to her being terribly rude to people. Her temper was often extremely short. I think that is true of anyone who lives in isolation. During the winter months out here when I'm seeing literally no one, I have no patience . . . I think that is partly the reason, but partly, it was in her character as a result of struggling so much. She would talk about Marin and how, "He wouldn't pick up my handkerchief, but I was the only one he allowed to hang his shows." She had a great streak about wanting to even up old scores.

She saw very, very few people, as far as I know. She would work in great spates of time. At other times there was absolutely no smell of work in the studio. And she might take to bed for two or three weeks—just lying there, saving up energy. I was taking Renaissance history at the time, and her position and her attitude reminded me very much of Cesare Borgia who used to lie in bed dressed in velvet, plotting.

Betty, who was at that time very close to her, told me that she and Georgia went down to the arroyo in front of the house in Abiquiu and burned six hundred or eight hundred canvases.

I think one of the things that was very clear about Georgia, too, was that in her own way she was carving out her version of a New England style. I'm not sure I can explain that; it's the first time it ever occurred to me. It was a complete marrying of stringency

and voluptuousness. That perhaps has to do with her ancestors. Most of O'Keeffe, I think, is a black-and-white covered wagon. She is the driver and the horse.

Interestingly enough, she became an American painter in the only part of America that isn't American. The Legislature of New Mexico was conducted in Spanish and English. It was the second-to-last state, before Alaska, to be admitted to the Union. I mean, she actually went away *inside her own country.*

She couldn't stand simply being known as Mrs. Stieglitz. It infuriated her. She would go to parties and they would ask her what she did; she would come home and vomit convulsively for hours, and, finally, she said, "I realized this was making me weak." She came back home and drew a tub of cold water and got in it and sat in it until she calmed down.

Here in New Mexico, she had superb health, ramrod posture. Her hair seemed made of gray. My impression was that she had become invariable, always wearing black and white, flat shoes, hair pulled back.

She was used to or wanted only the simplest and the best. She had a cook named Flora. I remember marvelous salads fresh from the garden.

The garden in Abiquiu, the house on the mesa, was one of the most beautiful gardens I ever saw. In pattern, I suppose, it would approach a Persian garden by reason of the fact that it was irrigated similarly. You have a grid pattern, and the water just flows into each of the channels you make. There were plots or plats, and the adobe wall. The watergate would be open in the evening, and she was magnificent—with a big black hat and a long black dress and a great white apron—very French, and very New England. She also served a very good Chilean white wine that she bought for ninety-eight cents and was quite proud of that.

O'Keeffe had few paintings in her Ghost Ranch studio at the time, according to Dash, but he did see a large painting of a tree. She had begun to paint the cottonwoods in the river basin below the mesa in Abiquiu; evidently, she had chosen to hang one at Ghost Ranch to provide a contrast with the dead tree stumps and shriveled vegetation outside the glass windows. Did the tree series have a symbolic meaning for O'Keeffe—regeneration? Roots? Immortality? O'Keeffe's tree forms were a departure from her usual language of forms, the ovoid earth and flower images, and the artist had varying degrees of success in her attempts to create a compositional format suitable for this shape. Her selection of the solitary tree may have been intellectual, dating back to Arthur Dove's use of the form as a natural object with transcendental associations—an earth-rooted plant symbolically extending its branches toward heaven. Her sensuous compositions of birch trunks at Lake George in the early twenties had elicited comparisons to Marlene Dietrich's legs, but *Dead Cottonwood Tree, Abiquiu, New Mexico* (1943) seemed more a paean to the virtues of immutable tranquillity. Now, in *Grey Tree by the Road* (1952) and *Winter Trees III* (1953), the new use of a soft focus to convey the upward-curving tree limbs admitted an other-worldly dimension. Dash's story is one confirmation that O'Keeffe was doing fewer new paintings at the ranch during this period.

The paintings that hung in Abiquiu were works she had completed much earlier. Dash noted, "One I remember I thought was a *trompe l'oeil* painting in a sense, that she intended it to be. It looked like a robin's egg on end, but it wasn't; it was a view of the sky through a pelvic girdle. And then one of the large black flower paintings."

Dash had probably seen *Pelvis III* (1944). Possibly he had also seen her most famous work, *Black Iris* (1926). These were undoubtedly among her personal favorites. In the fifties, she painted less than in any previous decade. Over the years, with help from Rosalind Irvine at the Art Research Council, her associate Doris Bry, and others, she had also assembled a complete record of her own creations. Dash recalled, "She had a scrapbook of what seemed to be, really, photographs of every painting she'd ever done. And I went through that. She had photographs and slides. I

preferred her earlier work. I thought it was more painterly. I think the desert is one of the most difficult subjects, outside of the Alps, to cope with in painting, and I think she literally *owned* it."

Her relative isolation, both physical and psychological, led to more self-derivative works in the fifties. Occasionally, in the past, she would take out an old painting, study it, and create a new work. O'Keeffe did this in the fifties with mixed results. *Black Iris*

Chama River Tributary

may have been "on view," but neither the form nor the style resembled her new iris paintings. In *Lavender Iris* (1950), the lower leaves curl together, and the central seed pod twists in an unusual manner. The flower is unappetizing. In *Lavender Iris* (1952), however, the flower is remarkably vibrant and alive. The lower tongue reflects the sunlight as the upper petals thrust out at diagonals that gently curve back toward the center. The two flowers from 1950 and 1952, one with a tortured, nightmarish quality and one that radiates life, suggest O'Keeffe's symbolic generation of her own garden, her own equivalents and self-definitions.

From the Plains II (1954, see p. 153) is a powerful and brighter version of her early oil, *From the Plains* (1919). The initial work's orange-yellow arc on black ground is transformed into a searing, jagged thunderbolt cutting a clean diagonal across the vast red-orange ground.

She also borrowed motifs from earlier works but used them in a different context. The ovoid clouds that had appeared in a few early paintings, such as *Palo Duro Canyon* (1916), reappeared in a new series, In the Patio. O'Keeffe began the series in the late forties when she was renovating her Abiquiu house. She made abstract paintings of the patio wall and her favorite object, the door. The walls were portrayed at sharp angles, with long, diagonal shadows created by afternoon sunlight, using only one or two colors, such as gray and mustard. *Black Door with Snow II*, *Patio with Cloud*, and *Black Patio Door* (pp. 132–134) each examine perceptual and conceptual distances between illusion and reality. These works do not contain the visual unity of the culminating work in the series, *White Patio with Red Door* (1960). The large size (48 by 72 inches) and scale, as well as the minimal design, finally capture the whiteness and sunlight of the imposing, protective patio wall. The simple formal elements—on a white ground, pale-red squares representing the patio tiles lead to a red door—have been linked to Minimalist art by many critics, including Hilton Kramer and Barbara Rose.[3] However, it

Black Door with Snow II, *1956, oil on canvas, 30″ x 18″*

Patio with Cloud, *1956, oil on canvas, 36" x 30"*

Black Patio Door, *1955, oil on canvas, 40⅛" x 30"*

seems more likely that O'Keeffe was presenting her simplified, peaceful world view in a literal sense. Whether or not she was influenced by this movement, the end result was not as cold, mechanical, and didactic as most works considered Minimalist. Rather, O'Keeffe had her own philosophy, carried over from her introduction, as a student, to Oriental art: "less is more." This concept suited her art, and, by extension, her life.

O'Keeffe also began a series, her most esoteric, reputed to have been done from tiny one-inch-square sketches made from airplanes during world travels. The titles are very abstract, such as those of the 1959 works *It Was Red and Pink, Only One,* and *Blue B* (see pp. 148–149, 152). The colors, muddied or overlaid with other hues, are different from O'Keeffe's usually fresh palette, as Lloyd Goodrich has pointed out. Also, the relation between colors and forms seems arbitrary and ambiguous. Ironically, paintings said to be inspired by the natural landscape seem, conversely, artificial. *Only One* may depict the horizontal sweep of a river, with two small tributaries branching into the land/ground area. These forms have a strong resemblance to the curve of the Chama River between O'Keeffe's two houses (see p. 131). Whether O'Keeffe was using local or aerial views, these works, like *Lavender Iris* (1950), seem to distort the clean shapes and colors that are O'Keeffe's trademark.

Although some Expressionist artists of the fifties and sixties were exhibiting works that were even more grotesque and atonal, their formal concerns and masterful painterly qualities were no longer O'Keeffe's. Mastery of the medium is what her new works lacked. At age seventy-two, her eyesight and manual dexterity were, naturally, declining. The works seem, again, not derivative of other art influences, but the expression of a personal mood or idiosyncrasy.

Like most of her other friendships in the fifties, O'Keeffe's rapport with Adams was at a lull or hiatus. From 1954 to 1958, she tried to convince him to print Stieglitz's photographs for a small exhibition at the National Gallery of Art. O'Keeffe did not allow the National Gallery to take charge of its own exhibition and catalogue because she understood the collection best. She put her assistant Doris Bry in charge of the catalogue and text and asked Adams to assist with the prints.

With her usual directness, she sent Adams several Stieglitz photographs without considering whether copying the prints was an imposition on his talents as an original photographer. Four years later, Adams made copies of a few prints. He recalled, "I made pictures of some of the avenues on Type 53 Polaroid film. Type 53 film had a very long scale, and the copies were very handsome. Ordinary films don't have that linear scale. I made them in San Francisco, circa 1958. It was quite a job. They had to be exactly right." When O'Keeffe wrote to him on October 20, 1958, she noted that the catalogue had a "good feeling" but that the reproductions were "not very good." Adams did not reply to this mixed message. In fact, the tones and details of the reproductions in the 1958 catalogue surpassed those of most later catalogues O'Keeffe supervised.[4]

It was not until 1961 that Adams took the Stieglitz prints out of his vault and returned them to O'Keeffe "in precisely the same condition." O'Keeffe, at seventy-four, had taken a July raft trip on the Colorado River. After she described the adventure, including a sandstorm and roaring waterfalls, Adams wrote back that he was jealous!

In an interview in August 1982, Adams reflected on his friendship with O'Keeffe and Stieglitz, "It was a very happy acquaintance." When asked about their philosophical differences, Adams explained:

I think I am more gregarious. I did not understand the high values that Stieglitz put on O'Keeffe's paintings but, you see, I could not work in the same way, and did not have the experience they did. He once said to me if he made twenty-five photographs a year, that would be a big year. O'Keeffe claimed that I was scattering too much and that I should concentrate more on my creative work. (Edward Weston said the same thing.) It was all very friendly. We are different in many ways, but the same motives are there.

Adams knew what it felt like to become a legend in his own time—and that O'Keeffe was in a similar position. So I asked him: "Do you think that O'Keeffe the myth and O'Keeffe the person are one? Is there a person behind the myth that's different from the myth?"

Adams replied, "For instance, I'm very well known. There are all kinds of apocryphal stories and exaggerations, and I think some of them are funny, and some of them are rather sad. I'm known as a figure; a lot of people never meet me and I exist in a sort of never-never land that people build up. But that's all right. They can't help it. You can't reach everybody.

"She still has a mystique, I call it," Adams continued. "It's automatic. She's just O'Keeffe. She wears a certain kind of clothes, has a certain manner. She's a very great artist. Nobody can look at a painting without being deeply affected. So the mystique begins and endures."

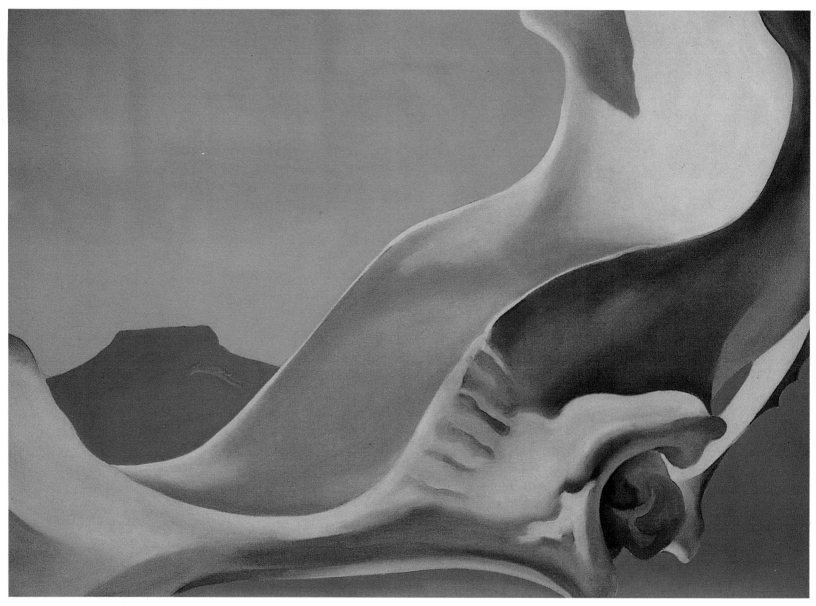

Pelvis with Pedernal, *1943, oil on canvas, 16" x 22"*

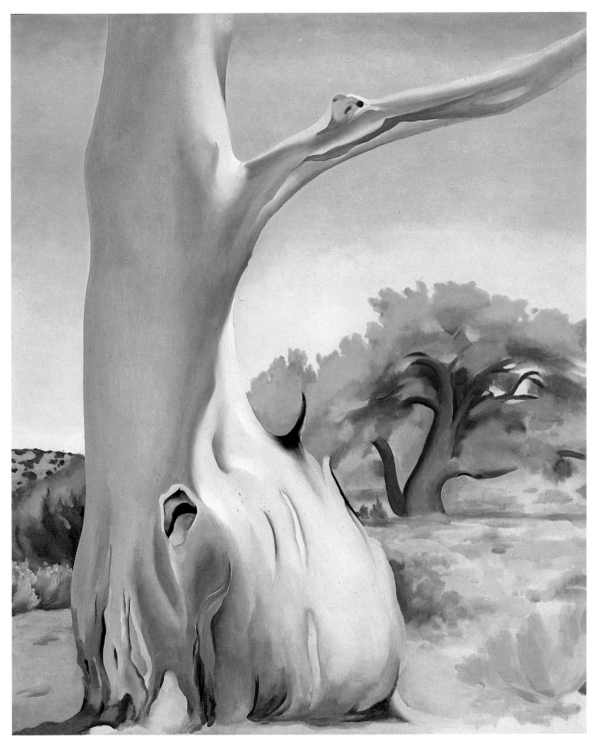

Dead Cottonwood Tree, Abiquiu, New Mexico, *1943, oil on canvas, 36" x 30$^{1}/_{16}$"*

Georgia O'Keeffe visits the San Francisco Museum of Modern Art, August 15, 1982, and poses in front of her piece, Abstraction, *photograph by Ben Blackwell, sculpture 1980, aluminum, 10'*

6. O'Keeffe and America

Throughout her artistic career, and especially from the forties through the seventies, O'Keeffe extended her long-developed habit of being in charge of her exhibitions at Stieglitz's galleries to include the supervision of her exhibitions at museums throughout America. Stieglitz had given O'Keeffe absolute control over the preparation of the exhibition space and the hanging of her shows (and those of others) during his lifetime, and this contributed to her adamant insistence on these rights when her works began to be shown at nationally recognized museums.

She personally supervised the hanging of her one-woman shows at the Art Institute of Chicago in 1943, curated by Director Daniel Catton Rich; the Museum of Modern Art in 1946, curated by Director of the Department of Painting and Sculpture James Johnson Sweeney; the Amon Carter Museum of Western Art in 1966, curated by Director Mitchell Wilder; and the Whitney Museum in 1970, curated by Advisory Director Lloyd Goodrich and by Doris Bry. In addition, O'Keeffe participated in the installation of the Stieglitz Collection at the Fisk University Art Gallery in 1949, curated by Art Department Chairman Aaron Douglas.

These exhibitions were the first in which more than a few works by O'Keeffe had reached audiences outside of Manhattan, and, as a result, leading private collectors of modern art in these cities made a few purchases. Each exhibition had a certain mystique, a certain style that added to the growing O'Keeffe legend.

The high points of the first three and the last exhibition were her early art. The Art Institute of Chicago featured sixty-one paintings, with *Black Cross, New Mexico* (1929), on the cover of the modest exhibition catalogue and an introduction by Rich that provided the first lengthy discussion of the artist's accomplishments.

The Museum of Modern Art's press release in 1946 announced that Director James Johnson Sweeney "has written the book on O'Keeffe which the Museum will publish concurrently with the exhibition" . . . that . . . "quotes from a considerable group of unpublished early correspondence—generously put at his disposal by Miss O'Keeffe—between the artist and her discoverer,

Alfred Stieglitz." [1] For undisclosed reasons, Sweeney never published the book. However, O'Keeffe enjoyed working with the gregarious Irishman, and the fifty-seven works presented at the MOMA, chronologically ranging from *Abstraction IX* (1915) to *Blue and Red Hills* (1945), featured a generous selection of her more abstract compositions.

Varied reviews of this exhibition showed that critics were still hedging in their attempts to discuss O'Keeffe's art. Edward Alden Jewell, in his May 19, 1946, review in the Sunday *New York Times,* saw a confirmation that she was a mystic: "It seems to me, as it seemed as far back as 1928, that Georgia O'Keeffe is in the ultimate sense a mystic. Her work, so much of it at any rate, is charged with a spirit of universality, even when expression appears tethered to what is immediate and finite." Elizabeth McCausland, on the other hand, saw more of the "importance of the visible world" in the current paintings. In a May 26, 1946, review in *The Springfield Republican,* she used the opening quote of the MOMA press release, "Finally a woman on paper," attributed to Stieglitz, to launch an essay about the Thirty Years' War O'Keeffe had been waging to abolish the pejorative myths about women artists. Prevailing myths were still being put forth by one critic and rebutted by the other. A meaningful overview of the artist's accomplishments was missing.

The exhibition at Fisk University to inaugurate the Alfred Stieglitz Collection and Archives was complicated by the lack of a satisfactory exhibition space. Her friend Carl Van Vechten was a good friend of Fisk's president, Charles S. Johnson, as well as a trustee for its arts festival. Aside from Van Vechten's recommendation and her friendships with writer Jean Toomer and artist Beauford Delaney in the thirties, O'Keeffe had no ties with nor demonstrated interest in the black community. Yet she was willing to give Fisk a sizable collection of works. Doris Bry and O'Keeffe visited the campus to make arrangements concerning the bequest and opening in the fall of 1949. O'Keeffe viewed the old gymnasium that Johnson planned to convert into a gallery and conferred with him about its remodeling. The ceiling was dropped and windows boarded at a cost of about sixty thousand dollars. The walls were whitewashed. The finest lighting and burlap-covered partitions painted in pastels of gray, peach, and beige were installed—at a cost the university could not afford.

Since there was no curator at Fisk, Mrs. Pearl Creswell, a Fisk alumna and member of the intermuseum council of Nashville, agreed to help with the extensive preparations for the opening. Mrs. Creswell recalled,

When Georgia O'Keeffe was on the scene, she worked very closely, and seemed to have great rapport, with the students and carpenters and electricians. She saw to it that the gallery was very much in accord with her and Stieglitz's ideas of a gallery—a place of utter simplicity.

Miss O'Keeffe stayed in the home of the president, but she was curt, not warm and cordial, to [Aaron] Douglas. She didn't have any contact with black artists. Her dress was austere. At the opening, she wore a long black skirt and a pure white blouse. She was considered very eccentric by people in general. The whole community of Nashville, especially the Caucasian section, was surprised that Fisk would come into the collection. [2]

O'Keeffe's gift did not include a fund for insurance and maintenance of the art. Furthermore, the "perpetual" curatorial fellowship from the Metropolitan Museum to the Department of Art at Fisk, announced by Aaron Douglas in his dedicatory speech, did not last long. The university lacked the resources to cover these unexpected costs. Subsequent damage to the building and the art due to leakage and humidity during a severe rainstorm caused O'Keeffe to eventually remove first her paintings and then the entire collection for restoration and storage in New York.

The forty-eight-page catalogue for the Fisk exhibition, with a foreword by O'Keeffe and introductions by President Johnson and Stieglitz's close associate Carl Zigrosser, had twenty-eight full-page illustrations and 101 works listed as exhibited. This was a significant art publication for 1949, slightly larger than the thirty-page Amon Carter catalogue of 1966, which had only seven plates to illustrate the ninety-six exhibited works.

The Amon Carter Museum's director, Mitchell Wilder, had hastily completed that catalogue, explaining in his introduction that James Johnson Sweeney, by then director of the Museum of Fine Arts in Houston, would produce within months a catalogue covering fifty years of O'Keeffe's work. Again, Sweeney's publication did not materialize.

Nevertheless, Wilder, with his museum's staff, compiled extensive, valuable curatorial records of all of the paintings considered for inclusion in O'Keeffe's largest exhibition to date. Wilder selected works from the artist's vaults in Abiquiu and New York, and from private collections. For the exhibition, O'Keeffe completed the largest oil painting of her career. The eight-by-twenty-four-foot *Above the Clouds IV* (1965) was retitled *Sky Above Clouds IV* by 1970. She personally supervised the transportation and handling of the works as they were being crated and stacked into the van in Abiquiu and as they were uncrated at the museum in Fort Worth. Again, the exhibition space was renovated at a higher than usual expense. The walls of the high-ceilinged main exhibition room were covered with off-white muslin. In photographs of the installation, O'Keeffe is shown wearing a simple black suit and her Ferragamo shoes, supervising the workmen and Mitchell Wilder as they reassembled the frame for the giant cloud painting and unrolled and retacked the canvas onto the frame. O'Keeffe, ignoring her usual attitude about not signing paintings, is shown writing on the backing of the canvas in her large, oval script: *Georgia O'Keeffe—1965—Above the Clouds*. O'Keeffe even retreated into one of the storage vaults with some paints she had brought, extending the edges of two canvases by painting onto the frames. At every stage of the exhibition, she had hovered over the art. More than ever her paintings were her children.

Sky Above Clouds seems symbolic of her large, yet enigmatic position as an artist in the sixties. O'Keeffe first drew her famous

Cross with Red Heart, *1932, oil on canvas, 83¼" x 40½"*

flat clouds in 1916 in the upper horizon of *Drawing No. 15.* The peanut-shaped forms contrast with rounded forms below, O'Keeffe's simplified image for cattle emerging from a canyon. The ovoid canyon is whiter than everything else, making it the focus as well as the actual center of the drawing. Flat cloud forms also appear in *Painting No. 21, Palo Duro Canyon.*

In the 1960s, O'Keeffe began a series of cloud paintings in-spired by aerial views during recent world travels. She sent for a large canvas, and when the delivered piece was too coarse, there was no time to return it. She coated the canvas with water, two coats of glue, and two coats of white base. The paint was mixed each morning in huge buckets.

In the completed work, *Sky Above Clouds IV,* a pink sunset spans the eight-foot horizon in the upper center. Flat forms iso-

lated from each other—the tops of clouds—diminish in size as they stretch from the lower foreground to the pink horizon and the clear sky above. The illusion of seeing the upper atmosphere on two levels at once creates a feeling of air, of space. The oblong ovoid cloud forms resemble the patio steps in O'Keeffe's patio series of the previous decade, as though the artist is presenting stepping stones to heaven. Although this work is not one of her

stylistic masterpieces and shows crude technique (with charcoal undersketch of forms visible) and execution, her diminutive figure as she stands before the painting (in an installation photograph) suggests the largeness of her vision—an airy, poetic, *shaped* immortality.

Her biggest retrospective was finally held in the worldly city where her career began, New York. In a 1982 interview, Lloyd

Installation view of the exhibit "Georgia O'Keeffe," May 14 through August 25, 1946. The Museum of Modern Art, New York City

Sky Above Clouds II,
1963, 48⅜" x 83⅜"

Goodrich, director emeritus of the Whitney Museum of American Art in New York, discussed how he initiated the 1970 exhibition at the Whitney:

I always felt there was a need for a big retrospective [of O'Keeffe's art] in the East. There hadn't been anything like this since the show at the Modern, and there was no catalogue in existence. Jim Sweeney had put on two or three shows, but without catalogues. Jim is an excellent writer; it was too bad that for one reason or another he couldn't do them. That was one incentive that I could hold out to O'Keeffe—to say that there would be a catalogue published.

So I wrote her a long letter and said more or less what I've been saying now—that we valued her so much, thought so highly of her, thought it was too bad that there weren't catalogues . . . It was a pretty eloquent letter. You're too young to have read "Mr. Dooley," by Finley Peter Dunne, a political humorist of the 1890s—he was talking about a speech William Jennings Bryan, the presidential candidate, had made; "Yez could waltz to it," he said. That was the kind of letter I wrote.

She was very interested. She came east and we had lunch together—around 1968—and she agreed that we could give the show. I had stressed the fact that there was nothing in print about her between hard covers. That, I think, was one of the things that interested her. I said I would write the catalogue. One other condition was that the catalogue should be in print a month before the show opened. We had never had any artist ask that before, but we were willing to do it.

After lunch, we came down here [to the Whitney Museum]. I wanted to show her the floor that was going to be used, which was our third floor. That's the second largest floor. I showed it to her, and she said, "What's your largest floor?"

I said, "The fourth floor."

"Can I see it?"

·So I took her up and showed it to her.

Georgia O'Keeffe: *head (1887–   ) by Gaston Lachaise, 1929, alabaster, marble pedestal, height with pedestal, 23"*

Georgia O'Keeffe Against One of Her Paintings, *1944, by Elli Marcus, photograph*

She said, "I want this floor."

"Miss O'Keeffe," I said, "it's promised to another artist just at the time we plan to have our show."

She said, "I want this floor."

So we gave it to her. We postponed the show for a year. I'm rather glad we did, because it gave me more time to work on it. She's a very strong-minded person, as you know. I was glad to get the largest space too.

She invited me out to Abiquiu, and I spent five days in her house. They were very interesting days. She's a remarkable woman . . . Five days of really having a chance to talk with her. She had total recall—an extraordinary memory. We talked about the artists we both knew, and the artists that she was particularly fond of, like Demuth and Hartley . . .

We looked at her work. She was working on the great cloud picture, the biggest one, the one that we reproduced on the cover of the catalogue and the book . . . [O'Keeffe liked to give visitors the impression that she was busy working, but Sky Above Clouds IV *was completed and exhibited before Goodrich's visit.]*

Doris Bry was very helpful all the way through. She was in charge of the O'Keeffes in the warehouse in New York and made access easy for me.

Bry, as guest curator, contributed the catalogue, a chronology, a list of major exhibitions, and a bibliography; she also supervised the printing of the catalogue.

O'Keeffe was too busy to read Goodrich's essay for a year, but she arrived in New York to assume a leading part in the hanging of the show. Although this practice was not followed by most artists, O'Keeffe did not question her right to supervise.

For the catalogue, Lloyd Goodrich wrote the most significant and scholarly piece that had been written about O'Keeffe's art. The twenty-three-page essay was written without any advice from O'Keeffe and without reference to previous reviews and articles. Goodrich had studied a source richer than the old clippings—

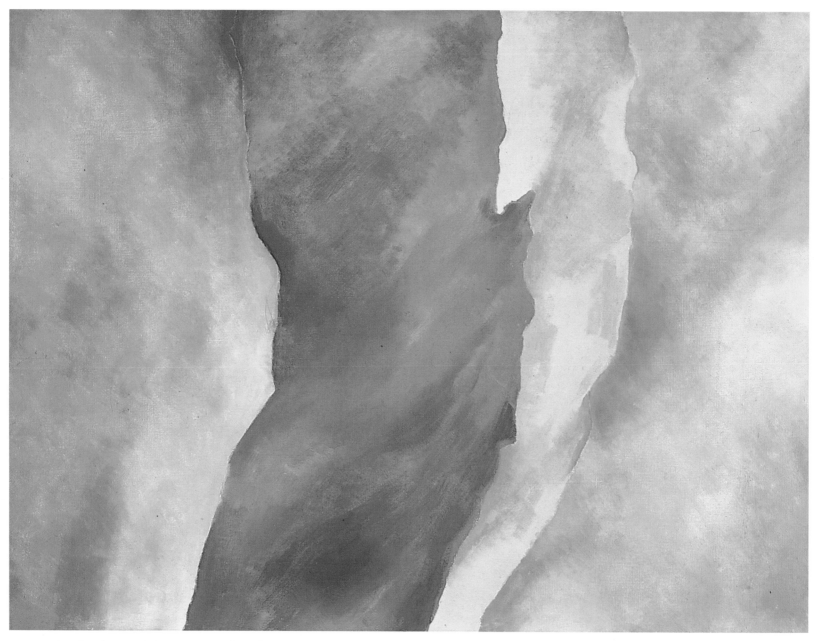

It Was Red and Pink, *1959, oil on canvas 30″ x 40″*

Only One, *1959, oil on canvas, 36" x 30⅛"*

the art itself. When he had founded the American Art Research Council twenty-six years earlier in 1942, he had selected several American painters, including O'Keeffe, and supervised detailed documentary studies of their works. The participation and cooperation of each artist facilitated this study.

The American Art Research Council secretary, Rosalind Irvine, worked closely with O'Keeffe, beginning in 1943. She and Stieglitz turned over gallery records to Miss Irvine and allowed her to examine, measure, and photograph many works of art. O'Keeffe was highly interested in having this record made, but she wanted it to remain confidential. Since Goodrich was firm in his stand that the council's documents were to be used for scholarly purposes, these records were the first and only ones made in collaboration with the artist to become available to the public in the artist's lifetime. Goodrich's interest in documenting many works by O'Keeffe provided the ideal preparation for assessing her art in a meaningful way. "I really didn't read the criticism because I wasn't interested," he explained,

I wanted to write what I thought myself. What she wrote about herself and her art was so eloquent, so good. It didn't seem to me that I needed to read what anyone else said.

Every phase of her work has been interesting. From the very beginning, when she did those extraordinary charcoal drawings out in Texas, which she sent on to Stieglitz—remarkable, really original abstractions based on nature. I don't see any influences at all in them from any other artist. They seem to me to be purely personal expression, all based on nature forms. Then there was the extraordinary series, the Jack-in-the-Pulpit Series.

It's interesting that she took such an emphatic position about her flower pictures not having any sexual meaning. I don't know why she took this attitude exactly, because it's perfectly obvious to me that there is a sexual content there. The energy is so explicit and beautiful. Then, of course, those days were more prudish than today. I think also there is an element of her not wanting others to

interpret things the way she doesn't want them to be interpreted. In other words, a kind of personal feeling that she'd like the picture to speak for itself and not have anybody read things into it that she doesn't want to mention herself. I don't think it's prudery on her part, but it's a kind of pride.

Goodrich characterized O'Keeffe's mystique and power:

It's a combination of extraordinary imagery and very personal and strong style, and an ability to project the canvas right at you. You can't miss the impact of her pictures. A kind of severity of style combined with sensuousness, too. She's a natural.

It's interesting to think what might have happened if she had never met Stieglitz. I think she would have gone, more or less, in the same way although Stieglitz helped her a great deal in the first place, in a material way, by showing her work first, then becoming her lover, her husband—and the contacts she made through Stieglitz with the other artists in that group were very stimulating to her, I'm sure. Yet she was still a loner in many ways, because she used to spend a lot of time up at Lake George even in the winters. Later on, she spent a lot of time out in New Mexico. They lived kind of independent lives, Stieglitz and she. They were deeply attached, I'm sure, but they could live separate lives. He was a very active man—influential, many friends, and the gallery was a very influential gallery.

Goodrich was enrolled at the Art Students League when he first met Stieglitz and visited the gallery at 291 Fifth Avenue:

I remember the gallery—how old fashioned it was. The elevator was one you operated yourself—there was a cable running through it. You were supposed to grab the cable and pull down, and it started up. You kept wondering if it was ever going to get there. [Elevator operator Hodge Kiernan must have been off duty.] The gallery, though quite small, was very avant-garde in those days. It had become renowned before Stieglitz moved uptown.

Georgia O'Keeffe at An American Place, *Fall 1950, photograph by Jack Holmes, courtesy Doris Bry*

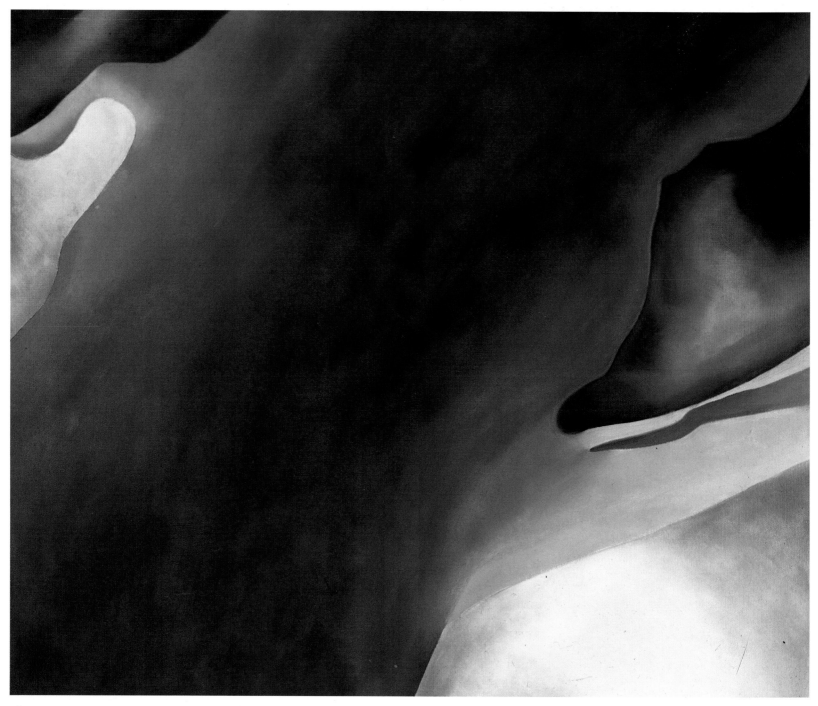

Blue B, *1959, oil on canvas, 30" x 36"*

From the Plains II, *1954, oil on canvas, 48" x 72"*

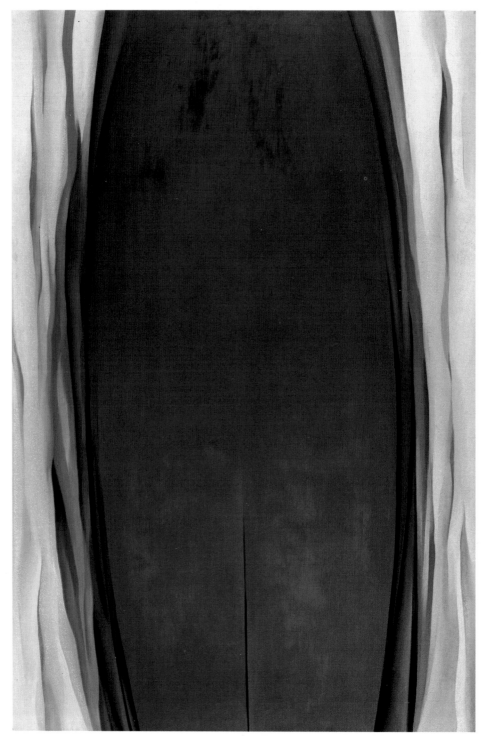

Green-Grey Abstraction, *1931, oil on canvas, 36" x 24"*

7. The O'Keeffe Tradition

O'Keeffe's early art education supplied her with the tools, and her early art supplied her with her own language of forms. These are the key elements that underlie the evolution of O'Keeffe's tradition.

As O'Keeffe was studying Persian and Egyptian design and avidly reading the art criticism popular at the Art Students League in New York, her perceptions about art were influenced by modern theories. Yet she incorporated these into the traditional approaches from her early art education. One formative influence which most art historians overlook is O'Keeffe's relation to the still-life tradition. Meyer Shapiro, in his respected book *Modern Art,* points out that when still-life painting was introduced in the late nineteenth century, it was a radical departure from (and no substitute for) the dramatic, realist, and transcendentalist landscape painting of that time. Schapiro notes that Cézanne took the existing conception of still life and adapted it to suit his own conscious and unconscious needs, transforming commonplace objects such as apples into personal symbols. Strong evidence exists that Stieglitz's early publication, in *291,* of the art of Rodin, Matisse, Dove, Marin, Demuth, and Hartley reinforced this direction for O'Keeffe.

Georgia O'Keeffe studied still-life methods and subjects—flowers, copybook images, plaster casts—throughout her early art education. She became facile and expressive with pencils, charcoal, and watercolors by the time she attended the Art Institute of Chicago in 1905, studying anatomy with John Vanderpoel. It was his insistence on meticulous, careful craftsmanship, not the realist approach of the life drawing classes, that she found valuable—studies of a particular bone or skeleton in relation to a specific, simplified ground. O'Keeffe's large drawings of bones twenty-five years later were an original infusion into this most classic of painting traditions. These bone paintings also used bright colors in one or two tones and hues, drawing on her acquaintance with yet another school, the Impressionists.

After her early art studies, the theories of Arthur Dow and Kandinsky inspired O'Keeffe to experiment, to go beyond and outside the normal boundaries of still-life subjects. As she returned to still life throughout her life, she painted an object so that it would satisfy the abstract criteria of line, form, color, and composition that she had learned from their theories.

O'Keeffe painted the traditional apples, grapes, figs, and pears that grew around Lake George; one new subject for her was leaves (see pp. 104, 120, 143, 160–161). Since plants and leaves appear in earlier photographs by Paul Strand and Alfred Stieglitz, their influence seems undeniable. According to one Strand scholar, O'Keeffe placed images in the centers of her compositions until she saw Strand's off-center close-ups. His use of textural definition and unsentimental objectivity, recognized as a significant photographic innovation by Adams and by Stieglitz, can be compared to the immediacy and sharp, close focus that soon became O'Keeffe's signature. Charles Sheeler, whose art included still lifes in drawings, watercolors, and oils, as well as building forms in these mediums, was in Stieglitz's circle in the early 1920s and was another indirect influence during this period.

Most important, her twenty-eight-year relationship with Stieglitz is seen not only in his sixteen hundred photographs of her but also in the eerie way that her paintings, in black-and-white reproductions, resemble photographs. Her close-ups of land forms, especially the hills of the 1930s, have human qualities that recall Stieglitz's portraits of the landscape of her body. Stieglitz's own advances in the art of photography were integrally related to a way of seeing that O'Keeffe shared. This was their most enduring tie.

O'Keeffe's own personal favorites indicate her originality and her deep concern with nature forms connected to life—shells, feathers, bones, hills, trees, clouds, sky, and stones. These forms were simple, self-contained, elementary, and timeless.

O'Keeffe may have been aware of the mystical and spiritual connotations of her choice when she began to paint trees at Lake George. The tree, a universally recognized symbol of immortality,

was a recurring mystical motif in the paintings of Arthur Dove, O'Keeffe's earliest favorite from the Stieglitz circle. The Japanese tradition of immortalizing certain hills, trees, and nature forms was introduced to contemporary Americans in Dow's composition books and in more rigorous studies by his mentor, Ernest Fenellosa. The honorific use of bones, feathers, and sacred peaks was integral to the Native American cultures. As O'Keeffe attended

Still Life *by Charles Sheeler, 1922, watercolor, 19″ x 15¼″*

Indian pueblo dances and ceremonies in New Mexico and visited their sacred ruins at Puye and other sites, she keenly observed the rituals and artifacts of the Indians, who still believed in the magic and powers of Mother Earth. At Ghost Ranch, the prehistoric vistas of the cliffs and the ancient Tewa peak, Pedernal Mountain, be-

came neighbors, conspirators in her drive to create.

When O'Keeffe moved into her second house in Abiquiu, New Mexico, she found *her* tree to paint again and again—an old cottonwood that faced her studio on the mesa. The fleecy, muted fall foliage—as human and fleeting as her own silver hair windblown

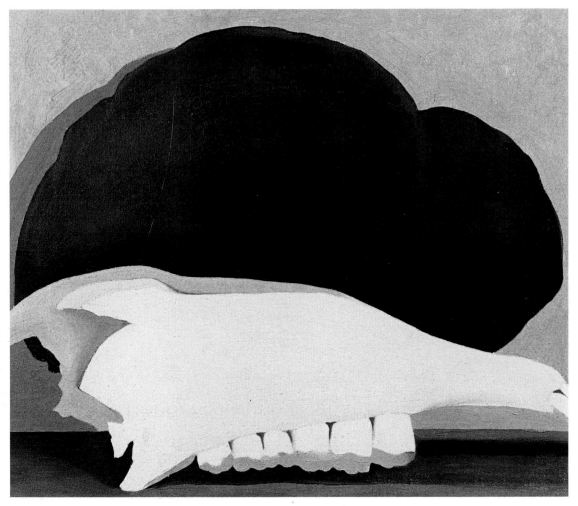

Jawbone and Fungus, *1930, oil on canvas, 17" x 20"*

Dark Leaves, *c. 1923, oil on canvas, 10" x 13"*

Large Dark Red Leaves on White, *1925, oil on canvas, 32" x 21"*

against the stark, bare landscape—was particularly difficult to depict in oil paintings. Some of O'Keeffe's paintings of cottonwood trees had otherworldly qualities that made these images different from the other works (see pp. 128–129, 163).

Her large clean patterns were her signature,[1] but there was always another dimension that defied logic. In 1922, she published a charcoal still life, *Single Alligator Pear,* in the literary publication *The Dial.* A lone, ovoid avocado faced its shadow on a pale, two-dimensional ground. O'Keeffe sketched and painted this shape over a period of months and decided that this composition was more satisfying than others with two or more forms. The fruit dried into a hollow shell with the hard seed inside by the time she finally "got it right." The geometry of a dark ovoid with its pale, elongated afternoon shadow below, within a lighter, two-dimensional square—a sophisticated version of an oval within a square—is the central focus. The avocado is in the upper center and the shadow occupies the lower center, where the traditional still life would be placed. The dark shape has the motionless grace of a stone and a "living" quality. The surreal overtones—the shape resembles a reclining, featureless head—are reinforced by the double shadow; one blue-gray shadow extends horizontally from the "chin" and the other shadow stretches vertically below. O'Keeffe's imaginative interpretation of the object and its shadow predates the advent of surrealism as a recognized art movement. The same intensity of focus and meditative quality occurs in the late paintings of enlarged black oval stones of the 1970s. The oval within a square compositional shape and pattern was repeated, with variations, during the fifty years between these two classic portraits. The 1940s close-ups of animal pelvic bones were the most original use, reversing the pattern to give equal emphasis to the oval hollow in the square of bone and blue sky.

O'Keeffe's early attraction to color developed through her love of the outdoors, a midwestern upbringing, and her early art education in girls' schools. Colors meant more to her than words. Critic Henry McBride would point out that O'Keeffe's color "out-

blazed" that of the other painters in the Stieglitz circle.

Just as her dialogue with forms became a versatile means of expression, O'Keeffe's color choices have undergone changes with time and place. Rarely straying from her preferred method of working with only a few colors at a time, she found many original ways to use color. Favorite hues were bone-white, sky-blue, and black, and the ochre to red desert earth pigments completed her palette.

Early watercolor paintings emphasize the light use of color, color separation between shapes, and the emergence of unpainted slivers and dots of light (see pp. 25, 34, 165). *Starlight Night* (1917) and *Light Coming on the Plains I* (1917) show how O'Keeffe used these techniques to compose her views of the sky working solely in her favorite color at the time, blue.

O'Keeffe also incorporated these watercolor techniques into her oil paintings. The color may be bold, but the medium, oil, never draws attention to itself. Brushstrokes are visible only in a few playful works, such as *Music—Blue and Green* (1919). In *Sky Above Clouds IV* (1965), the diagonal strokes between the clouds and downward diagonal curves on the upper clear blue horizon echo the sweep of the vista.

The other two watercolor techniques of color separation and unpainted slivers of light were not employed in early oil paintings but emerge from time to time, as in *East River from the Shelton* (1927–1928, see p. 73) and *Katchina* (1936, see p. 108). In many later works, the edges of bone, sky, and other forms are sharp and precise, rarely blended with adjacent color forms. Even O'Keeffe's trees with willowy, smoky foliage seem to have definite boundaries. One of O'Keeffe's compositional principles is that every object has its own boundaries.

Color is a problem in some early oil paintings. In many cases, the same coloration of an early oil painting, such as the bright red and orange in *Palo Duro Canyon* (1916), undergoes clarification of tone in later similar landscapes: *Red and Orange Hills* (1938) and *From the Plains II* (1954). The black outlines of the first work

Winter Cottonwoods Soft, *1954, oil on canvas, 20" x 24"*

Red Hills with White Cloud, *1937, oil on canvas, 6" x 7"*

and the subtle shifts of intensity in the second work give way to a forceful juxtaposition of clear, pure orange and red in *From the Plains II.* Yellow plays a key but smaller role in these three compositions.

In another early oil painting, *Orange and Red Streak* (1919), dark geometric background areas do not combine well with color. Both bright and dark colors seem too hard, vying for the eye's attention. One critic has pointed out that this harshness and disharmony were in vogue at the time. Nevertheless, O'Keeffe's composition lacks the dynamic unity and color clarity of her later work *From the Plains II.*

In the twenties, O'Keeffe eliminated black as outline and background and began to use black to create major shapes. In *Black Abstraction* (1927), *Black Cross, New Mexico* (1929), and the Black Rock Series in the 1970s, her simple, black forms represent different stages of experience and consciousness. In the In the Patio Series of the 1940s and 1950s, each shape has its own space and color and is adjacent to a white, blue, or ochre ground shape that is complementary. The color complements help unify each composition.

Along with her early attraction to color, O'Keeffe learned to simplify and enlarge her forms, so that her composition was dynamic. Whether it was the Dominican nun who taught her to draw casts large and light in high school or her attraction to the closeup photographs of Paul Strand, or, as seems likely, a combination of these, the design lessons of Dow, and Georgia's own style, her approach to composition was original. Moreover, many compositions from student days and the twenties were small in size yet large in feeling.

"To me, one of her fortes is scale," Sally Wilder, widow of former director of the Amon Carter Museum, Mitchell Wilder, has noted. "We were with Georgia a lot when she was getting ready for her retrospective exhibition at the Amon Carter Museum, and we purchased *Red Hills with White Cloud,* an oil painting done in 1937 that is six by seven inches. She compressed the vastness of New Mexico into that tiny painting. That is the greatness of that use of scale." [2] In the work, the red hills with one white cloud above reverse the long white and round red asymmetry of her five- by seven-inch close-up, *Peach and Glass* (1924). The interaction of the triangular red hills with the ovoid cloud perched above

Light Coming on the Plains I, *1917, watercolor on paper, 11⅞" x 8⅞"*

a triangle of sky has the intimacy of a still life, the geometry of a circle and triangle, *and* the scale that Sally Wilder has noted.

In O'Keeffe's most famous small still life, the five- by seven-inch *Red Poppy* (1927), the sensuous, China-red petals delicately curve inward toward the mauve and black central mound of seeds. The green neck of the flower head and the gray-white ground at the petal edges lead the eye toward the vibrant flower. The compositional features—a central, dark oval; surrounding triangles of bright color enclosed in knife-sharp edges of color; and pale ground—again show O'Keeffe's original use of the basic symmetry of circle and triangle. *Red Poppy* is an emphatic departure from both the artists of the Stieglitz circle and the Old Masters in color, form, and style, yet is classic in every detail.

O'Keeffe adapted and reinterpreted the still-life tradition, but her use of geometric forms, color, and a focus on a limited field and number of forms is rooted in the elements of still life and the photography of the Stieglitz circle. One currently held view persists in placing O'Keeffe in the realist school. Art historian E. C. Goossen hypothesizes that O'Keeffe's works follow the American Realist tradition of Copley, the Hudson River School, and Harnett. Alternately, Barbara Rose's thesis that she is an American Transcendentalist in the tradition of Thomas Eakins and Henry David Thoreau has a historical validity, but does not explain O'Keeffe's style. A third view, broader than that of Rose, places O'Keeffe in the Northern Romantic tradition.[3]

Eakins was a realist, a portraitist, and a rebel from the academy conventions of the nineteenth century. His work bears little similarity to O'Keeffe's in terms of attitude, subject matter, composition, color, or style. Her uses of abstraction, linear movement, and polarities of color and form have no overt similarity to Eakins's realist emphasis. The portraitist's studies with nudes got him expelled from the Academy; in comparison, O'Keeffe withdrew of her own volition from the life drawing classes at the Art Institute of Chicago because the realism did not appeal to her. Although her art education undoubtedly included an introduction to

Eakins's work, there is no evidence in her art or letters that she was particularly familiar with it. For their own reasons, O'Keeffe and Stieglitz adopted Eakins's attitude toward American art: "If America is to produce great painters and if young art students wish to assume a place in the history of the art of their country, their first desire should be to remain in America, to peer deeper

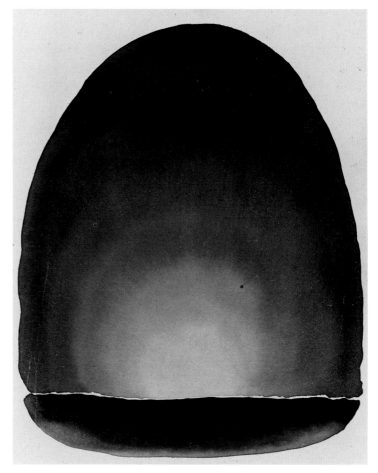

Light Coming on the Plains II, *1917, watercolor on paper, 11⅞" x 8⅞"*

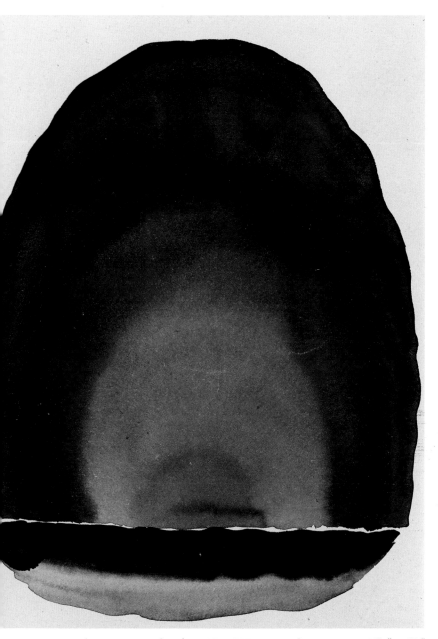

Light Coming on the Plains III, *1917, watercolor on paper, 11⅞" x 8⅞"*

into the heart of American life, rather than to spend their time abroad obtaining a superficial view of the art of the Old World."[4] Ironically, O'Keeffe began extensive world travels late in her career when her technique as an artist was declining. O'Keeffe's Americanism stems directly from the literary and photographic innovations of her times, as discussed in Chapter 3, and relates only historically to American artists of the preceding generation.

Similarly, O'Keeffe is alleged to have told Rose that she had read Thoreau, yet none of her letters mention him or indicate an interest in his transcendental theories. Did her values and her condescending attitude toward humankind echo Thoreau's? He had said, "Most men live lives of quiet desperation." Did O'Keeffe count herself among them? O'Keeffe did locate value in nature in her art, minimalizing the forms over the years, but she also steadily accumulated personal comforts: a housekeeper, a secretary, and a gardener, as well as black and white Cadillacs, Mies van der Rohe chairs, fine stereo equipment and records, frequent vacations in Bermuda, and world travels.

Art historian Robert Rosenblum has formulated a determinist, currently respected theory that painters working outside of Paris during the past century can loosely be categorized as Northern Romantics on the basis of shared emphasis on the archetypal and spiritual aspects of nature. Rosenblum argues, "Is the recurrence of Turner's isolation of nature's primordial elements—light, energy, elemental matter—within the more abstract vocabularies of, respectively, Rothko, Pollock, and Still, only a coincidence?" He places O'Keeffe's "transformations of primary phenomena in nature," such as the Evening Star Series, and her "vistas of primitive nature," such as *Red Hills and Bones* (1941), within this tradition. "Even within earlier twentieth-century American art, Rothko's symmetry and luminous emptiness find precedents in Georgia O'Keeffe, who, both in large late paintings like *Red Hills and Sky* of 1945 or in early small watercolors like *Light Coming on the Plains II* of 1917, distilled the components of a primitive landscape experience to an almost abstract image," Rosenblum has

Shell I, *1927, oil on canvas, 9½" x 13½"*

Three Shells, *1937, oil on canvas, 36" x 24"*

concluded. His hypothesis that these painters "seek the sacred in a modern world of the secular" can be applied to a study of the development of O'Keeffe's language of forms. Biographical and geophysical factors, as in many cases already discussed, directly determined her selection of particular archetypes.[5]

O'Keeffe's art, in the terms discussed by Rosenblum, can also be viewed as correlative with an even older tradition than the Northern Romantics. The sacredness of time, space, and nature is a belief that distinguishes religious from nonreligious human-kind, according to philosopher Mircea Eliade. Eliade amplifies Rosenblum's idea of the sacred by discussing some historical paradigms in his book *The Sacred and the Profane*. Eliade points out:

. . . every religious man places himself at the Center of the World and by the same token at the very source of absolute reality, as close as possible to the opening that ensures him communication with the gods.

. . . By assuming the responsibility of creating the world that he has chosen to inhabit, he not only cosmicizes chaos but also sanctifies his little cosmos by making it like the world of the gods. . . . In short, this religious nostalgia expresses the desire to live in a pure and holy cosmos, as it was in the beginning, when it came fresh from the Creator's hands.[6]

Did Georgia O'Keeffe, as an artist, place herself at the center of a sanctified cosmos? In some respects, O'Keeffe seems to fit the role of the sacred, rather than the secular, artist/creator. Her works seem to exist in a universal present time that also represents "the time of origin." Her works are composed of a small number of forms with ritual significance that inhabit a consecrated space. Her works contain a center of "absolute reality."

As much as this view could help to unify O'Keeffe's art and life, not all of Eliade's theories about sacrality may apply. Why does O'Keeffe deny the male and female symbols in her works? This issue, as discussed elsewhere, seems to involve O'Keeffe's determination to assert the real, as opposed to the symbolic, nature of each object. Nor did she favor the religious interpretations of the earth as a sign of fertility, a bearer of life and death. Her opinion about the significance of dreams is unknown. It is possible to conclude that O'Keeffe's world view does not conform entirely with

Light Coming on the Plains, *1917, watercolor, 17¾" x 13¾"*

historic beliefs in sacred space but that her art does! This paradox seems to stem from the mystique that O'Keeffe cultivated to maintain her privacy.

In fact, particular life experiences reinforced O'Keeffe's views of nature and herself. When the monumental Armory Show of 1913 introduced a vast audience to the Paris-based cubist movement, O'Keeffe was in Texas, experiencing nature firsthand. Stieglitz, by sending his first photographs of her to Texas, reinforced her experiments in art by bolstering her self-image and self-confidence. O'Keeffe began to paint nature to suit herself, transforming each object into art. Whether she was painting a flower or a canyon, she saw the image she wanted in her mind's eye—both the forms themselves and their abstract qualities. Unique vision was O'Keeffe's strength, foundation, and credo in her development into a great artist.

O'Keeffe's art and life may be seen simplistically as a series of upward-spiraling ten-year cycles, beginning in 1916 with her soul-searching correspondence with her friend Anita. The peak in 1926 was *Black Iris;* in 1937, *From the Faraway Nearby;* in 1944, the Pelvis Series; in 1960, *White Patio with Red Door I;* and in 1970, the Black Rock Series. With each decade, O'Keeffe added another chapter to her language of forms, making canvases that contained the style, balance, and endurance that elude most people in their lives. In her art, she was offering each viewer not the cloud-lined pathway to heaven but an extreme distillation of what can be seen on earth.

O'Keeffe's later paintings are meditations on nature, each form containing a reverberating simplicity. In *Black Rock with Blue Sky and White Clouds* (1972), the shining rock with its short dark shadow balances on a white pedestal before the daylight-blue sky. The blue sky forms curving hourglass shapes to sharpen the outline of the large black heart-shaped rock. The Japanese and Native American traditions venerate stones, and O'Keeffe's choice of the stone in a black, white, and blue composition is clearly the apotheosis of her vision as a worldly American. In the broadest sense, O'Keeffe's art speaks of the timeless struggles, the polarities, and human interrelations with the natural world.

Goat's Horn with Red, *1945, pastel, 27¾" x 31½"*

Afterword:
The Pursuit
of Truth

"I was born in Hoboken. I am an American. Photography is my passion. The search for Truth my obsession."

Alfred Stieglitz[1]

"To unify in the pursuit of truth is a natural instinct, but dangerous to truth."

"Good art shows the defeat of human wishes by contingency. Bad art falsifies the world so as to pretend there is no defeat."

Iris Murdoch[2]

O'Keeffe pursued her vision and art, carving new monuments from the shrinking, barren, magical, rainbow-colored wastelands of New Mexico. One paradox—the riddle of O'Keeffe—is that her mastery of her tools diminished as her mind broadened. Her eyesight shrank as her vision became more expansive. There is little public information about her eye troubles or the other physical problems that affected her dexterity as an artist. Writer Laurie Lisle notes that in 1971, at age eighty-four, O'Keeffe "lost her central vision and retained only peripheral sight—an irreversible eye degeneration found among the elderly,"[3] but does not mention her periodic eye trouble in previous years. Her eventual hearing loss and blindness in the 1980s was hushed up. In her later years, her public image has become that of a silent and majestic sphinx, elusively letting her art speak for itself. Her life and art have merged into one edifice, one artifact; in part truth, in part, the "supreme fiction" into which every public figure is shaped as a result of magnified, and, in O'Keeffe's case, carefully controlled, images projected by the mass media.[4]

The life that O'Keeffe has built for herself in the desert is indeed rich and varied. However, her apparent need to dominate others, to have her own way in almost every instance imaginable, has limited the depth of most of her human relationships. O'Keeffe's need to excise everything extraneous to her painting has brought luminosity and purity to her art but has often embittered or ruined her relationships with people. This may explain her seeming inability to sustain lasting relationships with others. The dichotomies between O'Keeffe's work and her temperament are not the focus of this book, yet the picture of her difficult life as a leading artist of her century in America would be incomplete without some examination of her failures in interpersonal dynamics.

She summarized one failing in the relationship with her husband poetically in her introduction to the Metropolitan Museum's catalogue, *Georgia O'Keeffe by Alfred Stieglitz*:

There was a constant grinding like the ocean. It was as if something hot, dark, and destructive was hitched to the highest, brightest star.

For me he was much more wonderful in his work than as a human being.

It is conceivable that Stieglitz might have responded in kind, but his silence is immutable. Others have been silenced more directly by O'Keeffe, both in and out of the courts. Three examples will suffice. Doris Bry, O'Keeffe's former assistant of more than thirty years, has been silenced in effect by a lawsuit brought by O'Keeffe challenging Bry's right to sell her paintings. (Bry's countersuit further delayed the case, which was finally settled.) Art historian Barbara Rose has also been silenced by O'Keeffe: publication of her edited sampling of the early Stieglitz/O'Keeffe correspondence, initiated and authorized by O'Keeffe, has been blocked by the artist's claim that her lawyers would not grant permission.

With Bry and Rose, whose motivations may have included self-interest, one might argue that the possibility of incurring O'Keeffe's displeasure was a calculated risk. But what is one to say about Anita Pollitzer? Soon after retiring in the early fifties from a career as an international leader in behalf of women's rights, Pollitzer, with O'Keeffe's consent, embarked on an informal biography of her lifelong friend. A 1955 letter, typical of the periodic reports she sent between visits to her subject and environs of O'Keeffe's past, exemplified her enthusiasm and conscientiousness:

October 22, 1955

. . . Some weeks ago I wrote to Dr. F. S. C. Northrop [author of] "The Meeting of East and West" in which he wrote a great deal . . . in highest praise of you—and used as his frontispiece your blue lines art & another abstraction as an illustration [Abstraction #3 (1924)]—He is Head of Yale Philosophy Department. He has lived in the Orient . . . scholarly . . . [I] read [his book] ten times . . . [and] showed him mine [the O'Keeffe biography] . . . He said . . . James Sweeney & Francis Taylor don't understand O'Keeffe . . . said glad you're doing this . . . no nonsense in his feelings about you. He sees the paintings completely—apparently he and Dr. Colbert and men like that see you as I do! Mighty fine feeling we have!

I told him that mine was a story of an American life—he liked my soil idea in connection with you (a little girl who saw dust on the road and sunlight before all else—and went on seeing it). . . . He told me you had given him a Stieglitz print which he loves—so you must remember him. Very ruddy healthy sort of individual . . . He apparently talked much with Stieglitz . . . liked 100% of what I wrote about the Oriental principles in your work![5]

O'Keeffe's letter of agreement in 1957 to allow Pollitzer to reproduce paintings and to quote her comments and writings was without reservations. In 1968, however, with publication imminent, that permission was abruptly and unconditionally withdrawn. O'Keeffe's reasons may have had merit, but her timing and her intransigence were a shock. Pollitzer slid rapidly into an early senility that required her care in the home of her housekeeper for the remaining seven years of her life.

Upon Pollitzer's death, O'Keeffe requested that her relatives return the two oil paintings she had given her. Since there was no written acknowledgment of the gifts, they complied; one was the well-loved *Single Calla*. One final irony: Portions of Pollitzer's manuscript—including the "buggy wheels in the dust"—would appear in the autobiographical essay O'Keeffe published in 1975.

Although O'Keeffe has not been truly reclusive and has often socialized and had visitors, she has been, in her own mind, very much alone in the sense that she once predicted to Jean Toomer. This impression is confirmed in the stark, carefully positioned images that photographer/filmmaker Victor Lobl found when O'Keeffe invited him to spend a week in Abiquiu in early December 1971. She had invited him on the strength of his photographs of Jacques Lipschitz and Marianne Moore, who had been a friend of Stieglitz. Lobl recalled:

The first day, the front gate was open; I went through and waited for her in her studio. A Spanish woman was there. O'Keeffe was just getting up from a nap.

I was stunned by her presence. She came from a bedroom in back of the studio and down one or two steps. I was waiting. She came out with her hair down—close to her knees, it seemed to me—extraordinary and young-looking, girlish and lovely. She didn't quite know who I was or why I was there. There was no urgency in the meeting.

Afterwards, I felt she had known who I was and why I was there. She was very quiet at first. Eventually, she started talking, and was very chatty from then on.

The first thing we talked about was the Vietnam War. She turned the radio on to listen to the news reports. The conversation ended up being about media—how difficult it is to hide from responsibility. In the past, if you didn't choose to deal with your responsibilities for the world's troubles, you didn't; now, there was no way to escape information. I had taken out my cameras and started shooting.

We went out to Ghost Ranch after lunch on the second day. The Ranch was closed up. She said she had been working on a painting at the house, of a rock on an upright cut log; it was in the living room. Just outside Ghost Ranch was the actual rock, and there was a slide of it at the Ranch. The rock was outside of her studio window, and she had brought the painting back to the house to live with it for a while. She was not actually painting. I had the feeling that it was a number of weeks since she had picked up a brush.

We walked outside the ranch but didn't go far. Her attitude about who she is is that she had left home and done well and that she was incomprehensible to the rest of her family. The result was that she tolerated them. She told a story about falling off the porch as a child. Her family had different sensibilities than her own. Something else was that she could relate to the outside world more easily than to her own family.

Another thing she gives off is that she has come out of a vacuum. Nothing around her can take credit for who she is. Her independence through painting eradicates where she comes from.

O'Keeffe occasionally framed things for me. I was very surprised by that. She would take the time to move something—frame it at her own suggestion. In most instances, it was not, aesthetically, what I wanted. My feeling was that it was her habit to constantly arrange things, to adjust them to the right balance. In her studio there was a row of tiny pebbles with a glass object. She spent a great deal of time lining up those pebbles.[6]

Lobl took photographs of her chow dog Chia, a buddha, the often-photographed snake skeleton enclosed in glass, five rocks on a window ledge, paintbrushes and spoons, two rams' horns, her empty white wooden easel, wine bottles, the record player, bookshelves, and art notebooks and files. Several photographs of O'Keeffe's hands show the artist's many facets: hands clasped in shadows, one hand in sunlight near her favorite Calder sculpture, and palms cupping a starfish shell. In Lobl's portraits, O'Keeffe looks into a straw basket, has one finger pensively at her lips, and stands at her desk facing her portrait of a young girl. One photograph of her head, at eighty-four, shows a wizened, unsmiling face lined with wrinkles and spots that are concentrated around her thin lips and between her slightly raised eyebrows. While it may not flatter the artist, it certainly captures her unflinching, uncompromising character.

Lowe notes that as far back as the 1930s, O'Keeffe's eyes had given her minor and occasional trouble in the category of that suffered by any normally visioned person who suffers eyestrain after painting for protracted periods. However, more serious problems arose in the late 1960s. O'Keeffe insisted on maintaining an illusion in public that she could see as well as ever. She knew the land like the back of her hand, so long walks and talks with reporters were no problem. What she refused to admit was that this was affecting her technical control as a painter. O'Keeffe had gone to specialists, yet was still not seeing clearly.

Declining vision is one reason for the scarcity of later works by O'Keeffe. One trial solution to the problem was not unusual in itself, yet O'Keeffe was furious when the story was made public. In the summer of 1976, John Poling was living at Ghost Ranch, doing painting and maintenance. He began to help with correspondence and other duties while her new assistant, Juan Hamilton, was out of town. One day, according to Poling, O'Keeffe asked him to "sketch a composition she had in her mind: a favorite view of her Abiquiu patio with a central door dominating the canvas and a row of flagstones below, similar to a painting hanging in another room at the ranch." Soon O'Keeffe enlisted his services as a painter, sitting in the back of the room with a pair of binoculars and directing Poling in the sizing, charcoal sketching, and painting of canvases. One painting that Poling produced working in this manner was *From a Day with Juan*.

When *The Santa Fe Reporter* published six photographs of O'Keeffe and her paintings on July 31, 1980, she promptly sued the newspaper for unauthorized use of her work—and won a nice settlement. Her wrath was directed against the publication's cover story, reporting that three artworks credited to O'Keeffe had been painted by someone else. The *Reporter* story noted:

O'Keeffe could not see the names on the paint tubes, so he read them to her, Poling said, and she could not see color samples on the glass palette they used, so he would paint large color spots on the canvas and she would approve or disapprove them.

Once they started work on the "Patio" painting, Poling said, they did little else until he had completed it about five days later. As recognition, he said, O'Keeffe signed her name on a little postcard, saying, "I should give you something."

When Poling saw that one painting he had done in this manner had been published in the December 1977 issue of *Artnews* (it was also featured in a traveling national exhibition), he asked for some credit. According to the article, O'Keeffe became angry, saying that nothing could be done, and refused to see him again. O'Keeffe told her side of the story to *The Reporter*:

When asked about Poling, . . . her words turned spare and bitter. She confirmed that the painting which has been called informally, "The Patio," and the two called, "From a Day With Juan" were painted by Poling, although conceived and designed by her. But she stressed that his contribution had no artistic significance.

"Mr. Poling was the equivalent of a palette knife," she said. "He was nothing but a tool . . . Since the beginning of time, artists have had assistants . . ."[7]

Although it is not unusual for artists to have assistants, as another article in *The Santa Fe Reporter* points out, O'Keeffe's pride casts a false illusion across her later works. Her need to maintain the façade that she can go on painting forever is "dangerous to truth" and "falsifies the world" in the senses noted by novelist Iris Murdoch.

O'Keeffe also began to produce pottery and sculpture late in her career. The late sculptures, with the exception of a fragile wooden piece, *Two Voids*, were all based on earlier models that were now sent to a foundry for casting. Museum Director George Neubert visited O'Keeffe to study her sculptures around Easter

1983. In a personal interview, he described her new pieces and discussed her sculpture:

She did her first sculpture in 1917 in plaster, a white abstracted form about 10½ inches high. She never let on to what the subject of it may be. But she said she was disturbed by the way Stieglitz had set up the photograph of it. [See chapter 2.] *She did another piece of sculpture in plaster in 1945 that is an obvious study from the pastel,* Goat's Horn with Red (1945), *at the Hirshhorn in Washington. In 1980, she had both pieces marked-up and cast at the Johnston Atelier Foundry in Princeton. The circular piece, titled* Abstraction, *was shown at the San Francisco Museum of Modern Art in 1982 at an exhibition of contemporary sculpture. She didn't approve the enlargement of the other piece, and as I understand, it's still at the foundry.*

At Easter 1983, I saw three new pieces of sculpture—conelike forms originally made in plaster and then cast in bronze in Colorado in 1982. The cone shape seems to come from the angled forms from the outside edges of the cityscape paintings of the twenties.

She's very coy. She gives answers that are enigmatic, riddle-like. Sculpture will be her last expression as an artist.[8]

Juan Hamilton, the tall, dark, handsome man who O'Keeffe hired as her secretary in 1972, had some training as a potter. His abilities to handle O'Keeffe's correspondence soon expanded to include business and art matters, including the coordination of her 1976 book, the biographical Public Broadcasting Service film by Perry Miller Adato, and with art historian Sarah Greenough the 1983 Stieglitz exhibition and catalogue at the National Gallery. Hamilton next became O'Keeffe's official agent for the sale of her paintings.

In 1977, O'Keeffe and her thirty-one-year-old assistant Hamilton were the subject of rumors that they would marry. Whether this idea sprang out of an attempt to end the legal dispute transferring control of the sales of her paintings from Bry to Hamilton or from the myth that O'Keeffe was, indeed, ageless, the two kept even their close friends guessing. On her ninetieth birthday, Hamilton and O'Keeffe celebrated with Sante Fe photographer Eliot Porter, his wife Aline, and Weston Naef, Curator of Photography at the Metropolitan Museum, who was visiting to confirm the selections for the upcoming photographic exhibition and book, *Georgia O'Keeffe: A Portrait by Alfred Stieglitz.* As their party enjoyed a Spanish dinner at El Paragua in Española, O'Keeffe had five margaritas and became very relaxed. Naef found O'Keeffe to be coolly elusive in regard to her personal plans, so, using the current gossip as his barometer, he called the photos he took during his visit "The Engagement Portfolio." Another friend from New York was invited to a wedding in Abiquiu and he thought it was to be O'Keeffe's. It turned out that two of her friends were marrying at Ghost Ranch.

Feature articles with photographs of O'Keeffe combing Juan's hair in the pottery studio she had built for him and informal, friendly authorized interviews kept the rumor in circulation. As late as April 1982, the cover photograph of O'Keeffe and Hamilton for *Horizon* magazine, showing Hamilton's arm casually around O'Keeffe's shoulder as he grasps a rung of the ladder at her house, gave the public another image, that of their close artistic partnership. It was no secret that Hamilton, by this time, controlled most communications regarding O'Keeffe's art. His association with O'Keeffe also possibly facilitated his own rapid recognition as a pottery artist. The magazine's inside photograph of Hamilton as a "Rising Star" in the art world featured the artist beside his polished, boulder-sized black clay pot in front of an O'Keeffe painting of the Washington Monument called *From a Day with Juan,* one Poling claims he executed. The article mentioned that Hamilton had married and become a father.

O'Keeffe has been truthful some of the time—to herself, to her friends, to the public. There were always different degrees. O'Keeffe may have described her own nature as well as Stieglitz's in the remark, "He was much more wonderful in his work than as a human being." O'Keeffe has remained a perfectionist. Her decision to control her public image as much as possible in her later years serves to exemplify the divergence that has always existed between the real person and the projected myth.

O'Keeffe's art should become known for a style that comments on and ranges between the various traditional genres. O'Keeffe's spaces, smooth surfaces, forms, and colors create rich, yet elusive, object worlds of their own. Her visual language, with its highly developed points of reference, must be further analyzed rather than taken for granted. O'Keeffe has distilled meanings from nature and herself on her quest for beauty in a profane world.

When O'Keeffe looked deeply into the sky and earth and translated their elements into forms, she found meanings in nature that eluded her in life. Her single-minded purpose was chosen carefully. If she made mistakes along the way, even as an artist, she has fulfilled her goal of seeing for herself and creating a universal visual language.

Notes

ACKNOWLEDGMENTS

1. A collection of prints discarded by Stieglitz that O'Keeffe selected, matted, and framed for study purposes.

1. BUGGY WHEELS IN THE DUST

1. Anita Pollitzer, *Georgia O'Keeffe: An Unauthorized Biography,* ms., private collection, p. 15. This unpublished 297-page manuscript was begun in the early 1950s with O'Keeffe's participation and cooperation. O'Keeffe wrote an open letter on February 5, 1957, giving Anita permission to reproduce any of her writings and paintings in the book. As Horizon Press was preparing to publish the work, O'Keeffe wrote to the press and to Anita on February 28, 1968, unconditionally withdrawing her permission for any of her works to be used. O'Keeffe, using strong wording, stated that the manuscript was sentimental, inaccurate, that she did not recognize herself, and that, despite their long friendship, she could not approve the work. While the book lacks the polish of a professional writer's prose and *is* sentimental in style, the manuscript, based on twelve years of research and writing, is indisputably a significant historical document. It includes some information directly from O'Keeffe and other primary sources that would otherwise be lost.

   Pollitzer's fifty-year friendship with O'Keeffe, beginning in their student days at Columbia University, is one of the longest continuous associations that O'Keeffe had with anyone. In addition, their early friendship helped to cement O'Keeffe's decision to be an artist and paved the way for her art association with Alfred Stieglitz (see chapter 2). This is documented in the letters the two friends exchanged, especially those written in 1915–1916.

   Many of the details that Anita recorded are presented verbatim, or in a more concise form, in the 1976 Viking book *Georgia O'Keeffe,* by Georgia O'Keeffe. This is a striking coincidence since, although both O'Keeffe and her former assistant Doris Bry wrote annotations to Anita's text, there is no evidence that they retained a copy. Moreover, O'Keeffe's comments in the manuscript margin, while providing valuable additions to the text, do not entirely discredit the facts that Anita presents, only a few extraneous details.

   In addition to correspondence and personal visits, Pollitzer researched O'Keeffe's family history in Wisconsin, visited Georgia's sister Anita O'Keeffe Young in Newport, Rhode Island, and did art research at the Whitney Museum, which has an O'Keeffe archive, and at the National Gallery of Art, which houses the largest collection of Stieglitz photographs.

   Subsequent references to this manuscript will cite the author, Pollitzer, and page number.

2. Pollitzer, p. 15.

3. This earliest influence must be added to later influences, of course, but has not been noted by most scholars.

4. These and other childhood memories are discussed in more detail in both Pollitzer and in *Georgia O'Keeffe,* by Georgia O'Keeffe (New York: Viking, 1976), n.p. There is a close similarity between descriptions of the "buggy wheels in the dust" and the "man on his back" stories in the two texts. Anita's letter to O'Keeffe on October 22, 1955, corroborates that Georgia had already told Anita the "buggy wheels" story by this time.

   O'Keeffe's account of the light on the dusty road and of being snatched away from light and freedom by her mother is a notable example of O'Keeffe's *selective* "total recall"—her consciousness of the meaning of this and other childhood experiences is obviously filtered through her adult sensibilities.

   Subsequent references to O'Keeffe's book will cite O'Keeffe in the text or footnote. The book is unpaginated.

5. Also described in detail in Pollitzer, pp. 26–27.

6. Pollitzer, p. 29. Also in O'Keeffe.

7. Pollitzer, p. 29. Emphasis added.

8. Pollitzer, p. 22. O'Keeffe's handwritten annotation indicates that she didn't remember her grade-school teacher at that time, over fifty years later.

9. Pollitzer, p. 33.

10. Story told by classmate years later: part of the legend.

11. *The Mortar-Board,* Chatham Episcopal Institute, Chatham, Virginia, 1905.

12. Lewis Mumford, "The Metropolitan Milieu," *America and Alfred Stieglitz: A Collective Portrait* (New York: Doubleday, Doran & Co., 1934), p. 33.

13. Mumford, p. 45.

14. Anita Pollitzer, "That's Georgia." *The Saturday Review of Literature,* Nov. 4, 1950. This article is retrospective; Pollitzer met O'Keeffe later, in 1914, but her statement about O'Keeffe's meticulous care of her brushes is valid throughout the artist's career.

15. Laurie Lisle, *Portrait of an Artist: A Biography of Georgia O'Keeffe* (New York: Seaview Books, 1980), pp. 46, 48. Lisle states that O'Keeffe returned to Williamsburg and that the family was reunited around 1912. Her facts are sketchy, and her interpretation does not accurately reflect the precarious family situation.

Pollitzer, p. 65, notes that O'Keeffe wrote to her Art Students League roommate Florence Cooney on August 19, 1908, from Williamsburg. However, it seems likely that O'Keeffe moved to Charlottesville with her mother in 1909, or shortly thereafter, rather than remain in Williamsburg. This biographical point requires clarification.

16. Arthur W. Dow, *Composition* (New York: Doubleday and Company, 1913), p. 5.

17. Wassily Kandinsky, *Concerning the Spiritual in Art* (New York: George Wittenborn, Inc., 1912 [2nd ed. 1928]), p. 45. This text by Kandinsky was published in New York in 1912. The title varies slightly in the 1914 London edition: *The Art of Spiritual Harmony* (London: Constable and Company Limited, 1914). The two variant titles account for the inconsistency between the title in the text and in the footnote. Pollitzer refers to *The Art of Spiritual Harmony* in a 1915 letter to O'Keeffe (see chapter 2) and O'Keeffe refers to *On the Spiritual in Art* in her 1976 Viking book *Georgia O'Keeffe,* which seems to be a remembered version of the title. O'Keeffe's and Pollitzer's correspondence in 1915 could be characterized as a spiritual quest.

18. Marsden Hartley, "Art—And Personal Life," *Artists on Art* (New York: Pantheon Books, 1945), p. 470.

19. John Marin, "On Himself," *Artists on Art,* p. 468.

20. Pollitzer, p. 75.

2. GEORGIA O'KEEFFE AND ANITA POLLITZER

1. Anita Pollitzer to Georgia O'Keeffe. All letters in this chapter are included through the courtesy of the Collection of American Literature, the Beinecke Rare Book and Manuscript Library, Yale University, and Anita's nephew, Dr. William S. Pollitzer.

Details not noted herein are corroborated by several sources.

2. Alfred Stieglitz published *Camera Work* from 1902 through 1917 and the more experimental *291* from 1915 until February 1917. "Underlying a number of *291*'s illustrations and literary pieces was a new freedom in sexual imagery, in varying degrees of subtlety," notes Sue Davidson Lowe in *Stieglitz: A Memoir/Biography* (New York: Farrar, Straus and Giroux, 1983), p. 196.

Both publications introduced O'Keeffe to the artists of the Stieglitz circle and provided important models that would lead to her own innovative style as an artist. Lowe also notes (p. 201) that the last two issues of *Camera Work* featured eighteen new prints by Paul Strand.

3. Georgia O'Keeffe to Anita Pollitzer, undated. Quoted in *Georgia O'Keeffe* film by Perry Miller Adato, 1976, WNET and other sources.

4. Pollitzer, chapter X, "The First Drawings," p. 94.

5. Pollitzer, p. 98.

6. Herbert J. Seligmann, "291: A Vision Through Photography," *America and Alfred Stieglitz,* p. 111.

7. Pollitzer, pp. 126–27.

8. Pollitzer, p. 129.

9. Lisle, pp. 116–17, notes that Francis O'Keeffe "was buried alongside his parents and brothers in the Catholic cemetery in Sun Prairie rather than beside his wife in the Episcopal graveyard in Madison."

10. Pollitzer, pp. 131–32.

11. The first work described in the "Evening Star" series, at the Yale Art Gallery, is simple and hazy in comparison with the works in the Museum of Modern Art, the Whitney, and the Amon Carter Museum collections. Both the technique and application of watercolor show increasing sophistication as the series progresses.

12. Specific texts O'Keeffe requested include: Sir William Matthew Flinders Petrie, *The Arts and Crafts of Ancient Egypt* (Chicago: McClurg & Co., 1910); Stanton Macdonald Wright and Willard Huntington Wright, *Modern Art, Its Tendency and Meaning: The Creative Will* (1913); Clive Bell, *Art* (New York: F. A. Stokes, 1913).

13. Personal interview with Mrs. Louise Shirley, Canyon, Texas, June 19, 1980, used with her permission.

14. Pollitzer, p. 144.

3. ALFRED STIEGLITZ AND GEORGIA O'KEEFFE

1. Based on information in Sue Davidson Lowe, *Stieglitz: A Memoir/Biography* (New York: Farrar, Straus and Giroux, 1983), p. 204. See Lowe for a fuller picture of Stieglitz, his friends and family members, his New York life, his summers at Lake George.

  Information that is not noted in this chapter will be found in Lowe, Greenough, and/or more than one of the other texts cited below.

2. Paul Strand's letter is used with permission. Copyright © 1984 The Paul Strand Archive of The Silver Mountain Foundation, Millerton, New York.

3. Lowe, p. 217.

4. Alfred Stieglitz, *Georgia O'Keeffe, A Portrait,* the Metropolitan Museum of Art, 1978. On the ninth page of the unpaged introduction by O'Keeffe, she states: "If they [several men] had known what a close relationship he would have needed to have to photograph their wives or girlfriends the way he photographed me—I think they wouldn't have been interested." O'Keeffe states in the same paragraph that Stieglitz "began to photograph me when I was about twenty-three." O'Keeffe was thirty in 1917, when Stieglitz took the first photographs.

5. Lowe, p. 216.

6. Lowe, p. 218.

7. Lowe, letter to author, March 14, 1984, and p. 219.

8. Lowe, p. 235; photo by Alfred Stieglitz, 1920.

9. Photographs discussed are from *Georgia O'Keeffe, A Portrait.* 1918 plates: 6, 11, 12, 24, 27. 1919 plates: 16, 25, 26, 21, 28 (in order discussed). The rare photographs of O'Keeffe painting are plates 43 and 44 in *Alfred Stieglitz, Photographs and Writings,* by Sarah Greenough and Juan Hamilton, National Gallery of Art, 1983.

10. Beginning of statement at 1921 exhibition at The Anderson Galleries. Cited in full in Lowe, p. 441.

11. O'Keeffe visited Alice B. Toklas and Picasso on her first trip to Paris in the fifties; on her second visit in the sixties, she chose to see Alice, not Picasso. She liked Alice's cooking and conversation better than Picasso's art. His similarities to Stieglitz would not have appealed to her at this stage in her life.

12. William Carlos Williams, "The American Background," *America and Alfred Stieglitz,* p. 32. Stieglitz's enormous influence on American art, literature, and photography at this turning point in his career is discussed at length in: Lowe; *Alfred Stieglitz: An American Seer,* by Dorothy Norman; *Alfred Stieglitz and the American Avant-Garde,* by William I. Homer; *The Collection of Alfred Stieglitz,* by Weston Naef; *The Hieroglyphics of a New Speech: Cubism, Stieglitz, and the Early Poetry of William Carlos Williams,* by Bram Dijkstra; and *Literary Admirers of Alfred Stieglitz,* by F. Richard Thomas. See Bibliography for full citations.

  "William Carlos Williams and The American Scene" was the title and theme of an exhibition at the Whitney Museum of American Art from December 12, 1978, through February 4, 1979. The poems selected by Dick Tashjian have the same painterly, closely observed imagery as the paintings of O'Keeffe and others. In this excerpt from "The Pot of Flowers,"

> petals radiant with transpiercing light
> contending
>   above
> the leaves
> reaching up their modest green
> from the pot's rim

  Williams is using words in a painterly way. The images, colors, and tones create a contrasting physical interaction between the basic parts of a plant, forcing the reader to see nature anew.

13. Williams, "The American Background," pp. 27–28.

14. William Carlos Williams, from "A Poem for Norman MacLeod," *The Collected Earlier Poems of William Carlos Williams* (New York: New Directions, 1951), p. 114.

15. The Pelvis Series of the 1940s is a more literal version of an ovoid as a pivotal center in space and time. In 1944, Elli Marcus photographed O'Keeffe in front of *Music—Pink and Blue II* (1919) (see photograph

in text). The two series are an interesting study of the artist's development of her own archetypal forms.

16. Lowe, pp. 248–49.

17. Lowe, letter to author, March 14, 1984.

18. The story about the lady and the flower painting is based on a letter in the Whitney Museum files. The actual letter is not presented to maintain the collector's anonymity. Lisle mentions this incident without citing the source.

There are many different feminist interpretations of O'Keeffe's paintings. Judy Chicago is one feminist who presents excellent points; however, her views, like O'Keeffe's, have been misinterpreted by many writers. Chicago told this writer that her art and views of O'Keeffe are inaccurate in the Lisle biography (conversation, March 26, 1980, St. Louis): "When the author said, 'When feminist artist Judy Chicago pointed out that O'Keeffe's flowers were symbols of female genitalia,' I wrote that that was not what I had said. I had said that O'Keeffe's flowers were feminist forms and symbolized one aspect of feminist art."

Lisle seems to be confusing Chicago's view with Linda Nochlin's, or blurring the distinctions. Nochlin's points about O'Keeffe's paintings in "Some Women Realists" present, as concrete, points that, to other critics, seem theoretical to the point of misreading the artist's works. Nochlin's view is quoted in footnote 23.

On the other hand, feminist critic Germaine Greer, in her study *The Obstacle Race; The Fortunes of Women Painters and Their Work* (New York: Farrar, Straus and Giroux, 1979), uses excellent analysis and methods to assess and interpret the political, social, and artistic positions of earlier women artists. O'Keeffe's position as a forerunner of many successful contemporary women artists deserves further study along these lines.

19. Phone interview with Myron Kunin, December 29, 1982. Used with author's permission.

20. Daniel Catton Rich, *Georgia O'Keeffe,* Art Institute of Chicago, 1943, p. 23.

21. Lowe, p. 289. See Lowe for further details of the complex family relationships at Lake George.

22. Lewis Mumford, "O'Keeffe and Matisse," *New Republic,* March 2, 1927.

23. Linda Nochlin, "Some Women Realists," *Arts Magazine,* February 1974, pp. 47–49. On p. 48, Nochlin states, "In O'Keeffe's *Black Iris* . . . the connection 'iris-female genitalia' is immediate: it is not so much that one stands for the other, but rather that the two meanings are almost interchangeable. The analogy is based not on a shared abstract quality, but rather upon a morphological similarity between the physical structure of the flower and that of a woman's sexual organs—hence on a visual, concrete similarity rather than an abstract, contextually stipulated relation."

24. Meyer Schapiro, *Modern Art,* p. 13.

25. Judy Chicago, *Through the Flower* (New York: Anchor Books, 1982), p. 177.

26. Chicago, p. 158.

27. Iris Murdoch, lecture at Washington University, St. Louis, April 21, 1972.

28. Weston Naef, "A Note on Stieglitz's Photographic Processes," exhibition plaque, *Georgia O'Keeffe, A Portrait,* by Alfred Stieglitz, the Metropolitan Museum of Art, 1978.

29. Anita Pollitzer to Georgia O'Keeffe, July 31, 1927; Collection of American Literature, the Beinecke Rare Book and Manuscript Library, Yale University.

4. GHOST RANCH: O'KEEFFE AND ADAMS

1. See Mabel Luhan, "The Art of Georgia O'Keeffe," mss., The Beinecke Rare Book and Manuscript Library, Yale University.

2. William Clark, "D. H. Lawrence's New Mexico Shrine," *New York Times,* February 25, 1978, sec. 10, p. 11.

3. See *Twenty-Ninth Annual Report of the Bureau of American Ethnology to the Secretary of the Smithsonian Institution,* 1907–1908 (Washington: Government Printing Office, 1916), p. 576.

4. Beaumont Newhall, personal interview, June 1981, Sante Fe, New Mexico.

5. Robert Rosenblum, *Modern Painting and the Northern Romantic Tradition: Friedrich to Rothko* (New York: Harper & Row, 1975), p. 72. *Church Tower at Nuenen* is illustrated on p. 73. Other works by Van Gogh that Rosenblum discusses can be compared to other images that O'Keeffe also selected.

6. Mahonri Sharp Young, *Early American Moderns* (New York: Watson-Guptill, 1974), p. 144.

7. The only copy of Cady Wells's Black Cross photograph is at the Amon Carter Museum, Fort Worth. An early title suggests that O'Keeffe

painted a cross on one of her trips to Arizona, but other information, in the text, places the cross near Taos. O'Keeffe did change the titles of her paintings whenever she got a better idea. Since she was using a composite of influences, the actual location of the cross is not as critical as the composition, which seems to be the same as that of the photograph by Cady Wells.

Dove's influence is suggested by Sherrye Baker Cohn in *The Dialectical Vision of Arthur Dove: The Impact of Science and Occultism on His Modern American Art,* DDS, Washington University, May 1982, p. 205. Cohn discusses Dove's interest in occultism and theosophical concepts in detail. On page 108, she mentions that Claude Bragdon, a theosophist and translator of Ouspensky's *Tertium Organum,* often breakfasted with Stieglitz and O'Keeffe at the Shelton Hotel, where they all lived, and that Dove probably met Bragdon and was introduced to theosophy through Stieglitz. On page 109, Cohn states that two central theosophical teachings are that life is immortal and moves in an upward spiral, and that there is a hermetic identification between the microcosm and the macrocosm. O'Keeffe was thus exposed to the kind of spiritual belief that Rosenblum finds in Van Gogh. Although she guarded her beliefs from public scrutiny, in effect, she put her faith into the earth and nature forms that dominate her compositions.

8. Lloyd Goodrich, personal interview on April 18, 1982, at the Whitney Museum, New York.

9. Beaumont Newhall, personal interview, June 1981.

10. Lowe, p. 322. Some information from paragraph that follows also comes from this source.

11. Photograph in *Stieglitz: A Memoir/Biography,* plate 24.

12. Wassily Kandinsky, *Reflections on Abstract Art,* 1931, p. 134; reprinted in *Paintings by Kandinsky from the Solomon R. Guggenheim Museum,* exhibition catalogue, Tate Gallery, London, 1958.

13. Edmund Wilson's phrase in a 1920 review.

14. Sidra Stich, *Joan Miró: The Development of a Sign Language* (St. Louis: Washington University Gallery of Art, March 1980), p. 8.

15. Lisle, p. 213. Georgia O'Keeffe's complete letter of March 5, 1934, from the Furness Bermuda Line, to Jean Toomer, is in the Special Collection, Jean Toomer Archives, Fisk University Library.

16. Jane Downer Collins, *Georgia O'Keeffe and the New Mexico Landscape,* M.A. thesis, George Washington University, May 4, 1980, pp. 63–64. See the photographs of New Mexico for actual sites painted by O'Keeffe.

17. The purchase price was fifty dollars, while the current market value exceeds eighteen thousand dollars.

18. Jan Garden Castro, "Interview with Ansel Adams," August 16, 1982, *River Styx Magazine,* no. 13, 1983, p. 53. Other details from this interview are included in this portion of the text.

19. Andrea Gray, *Ansel Adams, An American Place, 1936.* Center for Creative Photography (Tucson: University of Arizona, 1982). This catalogue documents the events leading up to the exhibition and traces most of the works exhibited.

20. Adams interview, p. 55.

21. "O'Keeffe Site Bill Passes," *New Mexican,* August 20, 1980, p. 1. "People," *St. Louis Post-Dispatch,* October 7, 1983, p. 2A, 5th edition. Senator Pete Domenici introduced both bills—to develop the site and to cancel the historic designation of her home and studio in Abiquiu.

5. BONE VISION

All quotations not otherwise documented in chapter 5 are from original interviews and are used with the speaker's permission:

Ansel Adams, Carmel, California, August 1980 and August 1982. Portions published in *River Styx Magazine* no. 13, 1983.

Robert Dash, Long Island, New York, July 25, 1979.

Beaumont Newhall, St. Louis, April 5, 1980.

1. Lowe, p. 377, and letter to author, May 21, 1984. The inference is that Dorothy Norman was sobbing.

2. This is the basis for the current Stieglitz Collection and Archive at the Beinecke Rare Book and Manuscript Library, Yale University. Peter Bunnell, then a graduate student, now is a distinguished professor of the history of photography at Princeton University.

3. Hilton Kramer, "The American Precisionists," *Arts,* March 1961.

   Barbara Rose, "O'Keeffe's Trail," *New York Review of Books,* March 31, 1977.

4. Bry, Doris, *Alfred Stieglitz, Exhibition of Photographs* (Washington, D.C.: National Gallery of Smithsonian Institution, 1958).

   ———, *Alfred Stieglitz: Photographer* (Boston: Museum of Fine Arts, 1965).

   Sarah Greenough and Juan Hamilton, *Alfred Stieglitz: Photographs and Writings* (New York and Washington, D.C.: Callaway Editions/National Gallery of Art, 1983).

All three books were printed by the highly respected Meriden Gravure Company in Meriden, Connecticut, and, although fine differences exist, the quality of the reproductions is comparable. The 1983 edition is more luxurious in terms of paper quality and trim size. The tones, contrasts, and details seem sharpest in the 1958 volume.

6. O'KEEFFE AND AMERICA

1. "Paintings of Georgia O'Keeffe Shown in Retrospective Exhibition at Museum of Modern Art," press release, Museum of Modern Art, 1946, 3 pp.
2. Mrs. Pearl Creswell, personal interview, August 1977, Fisk University, Gallery of Fine Arts.
3. Lloyd Goodrich, personal interview, April 18, 1982, Whitney Museum, New York.

7. THE O'KEEFFE TRADITION

1. O'Keeffe never signed her canvases on the front and only occasionally on the back. Some early and late works have a large script signature, "Georgia O'Keeffe"; in the middle years, usually a six-pointed star with OK inside.
2. Sally Wilder, personal interview, June 1980, Fort Worth, Texas.
3. E. C. Goossen, "O'Keeffe," *Vogue,* March 1, 1967. Barbara Rose, "O'Keeffe's Trail," *New York Review of Books,* March 31, 1977, p. 31. Rose states:

    O'Keeffe herself began reading Emerson and Thoreau when she was young, and there are so many correspondences between her subjects and specific texts by Emerson and especially by Thoreau that we are safe in assuming she was greatly influenced by their writings. Indeed her works so clearly convey the spirit of their loosely defined nature religion that they may be seen, in a sense, as transcendentalist icons.

    If we think of O'Keeffe reading Emerson's 1841 essay "The Method of Nature," her enlargements of flowers, leaves, shells, etc., take on new meaning as spiritual exercises . . . O'Keeffe also appears to have had in mind Thoreau's admonition that "Nature will bear the closest inspection. She invites us to lay our eyes level with her smallest leaf, and take an insect view of its plan," when she isolated a single natural form in a close-up view that filled a whole canvas.

Rose's view seems to be art-historical speculation; an exact correspondence seems unlikely. Influences that were contemporary and intuitive, however, may have produced the *results* noted by Rose.

4. Lloyd Goodrich, *Thomas Eakins,* Whitney Museum of Art (New York: Praeger Publishers, 1970), p. 32.
5. Robert Rosenblum, *Modern Painting and the Northern Romantic Tradition: Friedrich to Rothko,* see pp. 12, 201, 207, 214, 218.
6. Mircea Eliade, *The Sacred and The Profane* (New York: Harcourt Brace Jovanovich, 1959), p. 65.

AFTERWORD: THE PURSUIT OF TRUTH

1. Alfred Stieglitz, catalogue for his exhibition at the Anderson Galleries, 1921.
2. Iris Murdoch, lecture at Washington University, April 21, 1972.
3. Lisle, p. 318. Note also that O'Keeffe was alive when this chapter was written.
4. Wallace Stevens, "A High-Toned Old Christian Woman." Poem opens: "Poetry is the supreme fiction, madame." and closes: "But fictive things/Wink as they will. Wink most when widows wince." O'Keeffe was one to wink, not wince. She liked supreme fictions when they suited her.
5. Pollitzer letter is included through the courtesy of the Collection of American Literature, the Beinecke Rare Book and Manuscript Library, Yale University, and Pollitzer's nephew, Dr. William S. Pollitzer.

    Anita's letter mentions Dr. Edwin Harris Colbert (1905–), the distinguished curator and chairman of vertebrate paleontology at the American Museum of Natural History, New York, and author of nine books.
6. Interview with Victor Lobl, August 19, 1979, Williamstown, Massachusetts.
7. Hope Aldrich, "Art Assist: Where Is Credit Due?" *The Santa Fe Reporter,* July 31, 1980, p. 5. "Truth Vital, Experts Say," p. 15.
8. George Neubert, personal interview, San Francisco Museum of Modern Art, January 1982; phone conversation, Sheldon Memorial Art Gallery, Lincoln, Nebraska, August 1983. Mr. Neubert curated the sculpture exhibition at the San Francisco Museum of Modern Art that featured O'Keeffe's work and is currently the director of the Sheldon Memorial Art Gallery.

Selected Bibliography

COMPILED BY BETSY CONNELL

Adato, Perry Miller, producer/director. *Georgia O'Keeffe.* WNET 13, Boston. November 19, 1974.

Aldrich, Hope. "Art Assist: Where Is Credit Due?" *Sante Fe Reporter,* vol. 7, no. 6, July 31, 1980, pp. 4–5, 14–15.

———. "Truth Vital, Experts Say." *Sante Fe Reporter,* July 31, 1980, pp. 5, 15.

"The Art of Being O'Keeffe." *New York Times Magazine,* November 13, 1977, pp. 44–45.

Asbury, Edith Evans. "Georgia O'Keeffe Is Involved in Two Suits Linked to Agent Fees on Her Paintings." *New York Times,* November 20, 1978, sec. B, p. 10.

———. "Silent Desert Still Charms Georgia O'Keeffe, Near 81." *New York Times,* November 2, 1968, p. 39.

"Austere Stripper." *Time,* May 27, 1946.

Bovi, Arturo. *Kandinsky.* London: Hamlyn, 1971.

Bry, Doris. *Alfred Stieglitz: Photographer.* Boston: Museum of Fine Arts, 1965.

———. "Georgia O'Keeffe." *American Association of University Women.* 45, no. 2 (January 1952), pp. 79–80.

Castro, Jan Garden. "Georgia O'Keeffe." *Feminist Art Journal,* 1977.

———. "'Portrait of an Artist': Superficial Treatment of Georgia O'Keeffe." *St. Louis Post-Dispatch,* April 6, 1980, sec. B, p. 5.

Chatham Episcopal Institute Yearbook. Chatham, Virginia: Chatham Episcopal Institute, 1905.

Chicago, Judy. *Through the Flower.* Anchor-Doubleday, 1982.

Collins, Jane Downer. "Georgia O'Keeffe and the New Mexico Landscape." Masters thesis (1980), George Washington University.

Crimp, Douglas. "Georgia Is a State of Mind." *Artnews,* October 1970, pp. 45–51, 84–85.

Crowninshield, Frank. "A Series of American Artists—in color: No. 1—Georgia O'Keeffe." *Vanity Fair,* April 1932, pp. 40–41.

Daniels, Mary. "The Magical Mistress of Ghost Ranch, New Mexico." *Chicago Tribune,* November 24, 1973, Art sec., pp. 1–2.

Dijkstra, Bram. *The Hieroglyphics of a New Speech: Cubism, Stieglitz and the Early Poetry of William Carlos Williams.* Princeton: Princeton University Press, 1969.

Dow, Arthur W. *Composition.* New York: Doubleday, Page & Co., 1913.

Eldredge, Charles Child, III. *Georgia O'Keeffe: The Development of an American Modern.* Dissertation, University of Minnesota, 1971.

Eyrich, Claire. "O'Keeffe Show Spans 50 Years." *Fort Worth Star-Telegram,* March 18, 1966.

Fisher, William Murrell. "The Georgia O'Keeffe Drawings and Paintings at '291.'" *Camera Work,* No. 49–50, June 1917, p. 5.

"Fisk University Dedicates Alfred Stieglitz Collection." *The Crisis,* March 1950.

Frank, Waldo, Lewis Mumford, Dorothy Norman, Paul Rosenfeld, and Harold Rugg. *America and Alfred Stieglitz: A Collective Portrait.* New York: The Literary Guild, Doubleday, Doran & Co., 1934.

Fraser, C. Gerald. "Georgia O'Keeffe Loses Stolen-Paintings Lawsuit." *New York Times,* July 16, 1978, p. 43.

"Gallery Previews in New York." *Pictures on Exhibit,* 8 (June 1946), p. 12.

"Georgia O'Keeffe: The American Southwest." *Art in America,* January 1979, pp. 80–81, 107.

Getlein, Frank. "In the Light of Georgia O'Keeffe." *New Republic,* November 7, 1960.

Goossen, E. C. "Georgia O'Keeffe." *Vogue,* March 1967, pp. 174–79, 221.

Gibbs, Jo. "The Modern Honors First Woman—O'Keeffe." *Art Digest,* June 1, 1946, p. 6.

Glueck, Grace. "Art People: Miss O'Keeffe and Friend." *New York Times,* November 17, 1978.

Hamilton, George Heard. "The Alfred Stieglitz Collection." *Metropolitan Museum Journal,* no. 3 (1970), 371–90.

Hartley, Marsden. *Adventures in the Arts.* New York: Boni & Liveright, 1921.

———. "Art—And Personal Life." In *Artists on Art,* ed. Robert J. Goldwater and Marco Treves. New York: Pantheon Books, 1945, pp. 469–71.

Hillerman, Anne. "A Visit with Art's First Lady." *New Mexican,* November 13, 1977, p. 14.

Hobhouse, Janet. "The Artist Behind the Canvas." Review of *Portrait of an Artist: A Biography of Georgia O'Keeffe,* by Laurie Lisle. *New York Times Book Review,* May 11, 1980, pp. 13, 35.

Hoffman, Katherine Ann. "A Study of the Art of Georgia O'Keeffe." Dissertation, New York University, 1976.

Hollis, Janette. "Two American Women in Art—O'Keeffe and Cassatt." *Delphian Quarterly,* April 1945, pp. 7–10, 15.

Homer, William Innes. *Alfred Stieglitz and the American Avant-Garde.* Boston: New York Graphic Society, 1979.

Hunter, Vernon. "A Note on Georgia O'Keeffe." *Contemporary Arts,* November–December 1932.

Janos, Leo. "Georgia O'Keeffe at Eighty-Four." *Atlantic Monthly,* October 1971, pp. 114–17.

Jewell, Edward Alden. "Georgia O'Keeffe Gives an Art Show." *New York Times,* January 7, 1936, p. 17.

———. "O'Keeffe: 30 Years." *New York Times,* May 19, 1946, p. 6X.

Kandinsky, Wassily. *Concerning the Spiritual in Art.* New York: George Wittenborn, Inc., 1912.

———. "Reflection of Abstract Art." *Paintings by Kandinsky from the Solomon R. Guggenheim Museum.* London: The Tate Gallery, 1958.

Klein, Jerome. "O'Keeffe Works Highly Spirited." *New York Post,* January 11, 1936.

Kotz, Mary Lunn. "A Day with Georgia O'Keeffe." *Artnews,* December 1977, pp. 36–45.

Kramer, Hilton. "The American Precisionists." *Arts,* March 1961, pp. 32–37.

———. "Stieglitz's 'Portrait of O'Keeffe' at Met." *New York Times,* November 24, 1978, pp. 1, 14.

Kuh, Katherine. *The Artist's Voice: Talks with Seventeen Artists.* New York: Harper and Row, 1962.

Kuther, Janet. "The Grand Lady of Art." *Dallas Morning News,* November 13, 1977, p. 6.

Lisle, Laurie. *Portrait of an Artist: A Biography of Georgia O'Keeffe.* New York: Seaview Books, 1980.

Lowe, Sue Davidson. *Stieglitz: A Memoir/Biography.* Farrar, Straus and Giroux, 1983.

Luhan, Mabel Dodge. "The Art of Georgia O'Keeffe." The Beinecke Rare Book and Manuscript Library, Yale University, New Haven, Connecticut.

———. "Georgia O'Keeffe in Taos." *Creative Art,* June 1931, pp. 406–10.

———. *Taos and Its Artists.* New York: Duell, Sloan & Pearce, 1947.

Marandel, J. Patrice. "Lettre de New York." *Art International,* December 1970.

Marin, John. "On Himself." In *Artists on Art,* ed. Robert J. Goldwater and Marco Treves. New York: Pantheon Books, 1945, pp. 466–68.

Marvel, Bill. "Georgia O'Keeffe's World: She Re-creates an Awesome Nature." *National Observer,* October 19, 1970, pp. 1, 9.

McBride, Henry. "Georgia O'Keeffe's Exhibition." *New York Sun,* January 14, 1933.

———. "Sign of the Cross." *New York Sun,* February 8, 1930.

McCausland, Elizabeth. "Georgia O'Keeffe." *Parnassus,* March 1940.

———. "Georgia O'Keeffe in a Retrospective Exhibition." *Springfield* [Mass.] *Sunday Union and Republican,* May 26, 1946, p. 6C.

Mumford, Lewis. "The Art Galleries: Autobiographies in Paint." *The New Yorker,* January 18, 1936.

———. "The Metropolitan Milieu." In *America and Alfred Stieglitz, A Collective Portrait,* ed. Frank Waldo et al. New York: The Literary Guild, Doubleday, Doran & Co., 1934.

———. "O'Keeffe and Matisse." *New Republic,* March 2, 1927, p. 41.

Myers, Constance Ashton. "Pollitzer, Anita Lily," in *Notable American Women: The Modern Period,* ed. Barbara Licherman and Carol Hurd Green. Cambridge, Mass.: Belknap Press, 1980, pp. 551–52.

Naef, Weston J. *The Collection of Alfred Stieglitz: Fifty Pioneers of American Photography.* New York: Metropolitan Museum of Art and The Viking Press, 1978.

Nochlin, Linda. "Some Women Realists." *Arts,* February 1974, pp. 47–49.

Norman, Dorothy. *Alfred Stieglitz: An American Seer.* New York: Random House, 1973.

Northrup, F. S. C. *The Meeting of East and West.* New York: The Macmillan Co., 1947.

O'Keeffe, Georgia. "A Letter from Georgia O'Keeffe." *Magazine of Art,* no. 37 (February 1944), p. 70.

———. *Georgia O'Keeffe.* New York: Viking, 1976.

———. *Georgia O'Keeffe Drawings.* Introduction by Lloyd Goodrich. [Limited edition of ten drawing reproductions signed and numbered by the artist.] New York: Atlantis Editions, 1968.

———. *Some Memories of Drawings.* [Limited edition of twenty-one drawing reproductions with text by the artist and signed by her.] New York: Atlantis Editions, 1974.

"O'Keeffe's Pineapple." *Art Digest,* February 15, 1940, p. 23.

"O'Keeffe Site Bill Passes." *New Mexican,* August 20, 1980, p. 1.

"O'Keeffe Wins Edward MacDowell Medal." *St. Louis Post-Dispatch,* August 16, 1972.

Peters, Sarah W. "Georgia O'Keeffe." In *Women Artists: 1550–1950,* ed. Ann Sutherland Harris and Linda Nochlin. Los Angeles: Los Angeles County Museum of Art; New York: Alfred A. Knopf, 1976, pp. 300–306, 358–59.

Pollitzer, Anita. *Georgia O'Keeffe: An Unauthorized Biography.* Unpublished.

———. "That's Georgia." *Saturday Review of Literature,* November 4, 1950, pp. 41–43.

Pollock, Duncan. "Artists of Taos and Sante Fe." *Artnews,* January 19, 1974, pp. 13–32.

Read, Helen Appleton. "Georgia O'Keeffe—Woman Artist Whose Art Is Sincerely Feminine." *Brooklyn Eagle,* March 2, 1924.

Reich, Sheldon. "John Marin and the Piercing Light of Taos." *Artnews,* January 19, 1974, pp. 16–17.

Rich, Daniel Catton. "The New O'Keeffes." *Magazine of Art,* March 1944, pp. 110–11.

Rose, Barbara. "Georgia O'Keeffe: Paintings of the Sixties." *Artforum,* November 1970, pp. 42–46.

———. "O'Keeffe's Trail." *New York Review of Books,* March 31, 1977, pp. 29–30.

Rosen, Charles, and Henri Zerner. "What Is, and Is Not, Realism?" *New York Review of Books,* February 18, 1982, pp. 21, 26.

Rosenblum, Robert. *Modern Painting and the Northern Tradition: Friederich to Rothko.* New York: Harper and Row, 1975.

Rosenfeld, Paul. "American Painting." *The Dial,* no. 71, December 1921, pp. 649–70.

———. "The Paintings of Georgia O'Keeffe," *Vanity Fair,* October 1922, pp. 56, 112, 114.

———. *Port of New York: Essays on Fourteen American Moderns.* New York: Harcourt, Brace and Co., 1924.

Schwartz, Sanford. "Georgia O'Keeffe Writes a Book." *The New Yorker,* August 28, 1978, pp. 87–90, 93.

Seiberling, Dorothy. "Horizons of a Pioneer." *Life,* March 1, 1968.

Seldis, Henry. "Georgia O'Keeffe at 78: Tough-Minded Romantic." *Los Angeles Times West Coast Magazine,* January 22, 1967.

Seligmann, Herbert J. "291: A Vision Through Photography." In *America and Alfred Stieglitz: A Collective Portrait,* ed. Waldo Frank et al. New York: The Literary Guild, Doubleday, Doran & Co., 1934.

Shapiro, Meyer. *Modern Art.* New York: George Braziller, 1979.

Stitch, Sidra. *Joan Miró: The Development of Sign Language.* St. Louis: Washington University Gallery of Art, 1980.

Tomkins, Calvin. "The Rose in the Eye Looked Pretty Fine." *The New Yorker,* March 4, 1974, pp. 40–66.

Tryk, Sheila. "O'Keeffe: 'My Time . . . My World.'" *New Mexico,* January/February 1973, pp. 18–23.

Tucker, Glen. "The Art Scene." *San Antonio Light,* October 19, 1975, p. 3.

Wallach, Amei. "Under a Western Sky." *Horizon,* December 1977, pp. 24–31.

Willard, Charlotte. "Georgia O'Keeffe." *Art in America,* October 19, 1963, pp. 92–96.

Williams, William Carlos. "The American Background." In *America and Alfred Stieglitz: A Collective Portrait,* ed. Waldo Frank et al. New York: The Literary Guild, Doubleday, Doran & Co., 1934.

Wilson, Edmund. "Stieglitz Exhibition ["Seven Americans"] at the Anderson Galleries." *New Republic,* March 18, 1925, pp. 97–98.

———. "Wonderful Emptiness." *Time,* October 24, 1960.

Young, Mahonri Sharp. *Early American Moderns.* New York: Watson-Guptill, 1974.

Index